RIGHTS AND REALITIES

Rights and Realities

The Judicial Impact of the *Canadian Charter of Rights and Freedoms* on Education, Case Law and Political Jurisprudence

JONATHAN L. BLACK-BRANCH MA (OXON)
B.A., B.Ed., B.G.S., LL.B. (Hons), M.Ed., M.A., Ph.D., ACIArb.
Wolfson College, Oxford University

Ashgate

DARTMOUTH

Aldershot • Brookfield USA • Singapore • Sydney

Published by
Dartmouth Publishing Company Limited
Ashgate Publishing Limited
Gower House
Croft Road
Aldershot
Hants GU11 3HR
England

Ashgate Publishing Company
Old Post Road
Brookfield
Vermont 05036
USA

British Library Cataloguing in Publication Data
Black-Branch, Jonathan L.
    Rights and realities : the judicial impact of the Canadian Charter
    of Rights and Freedoms on education, case law and political
    jurisprudence
    1.Canada - Constitutional law
    I.Title
    342.7'1

Library of Congress Cataloging-in-Publication Data
Black-Branch, Jonathan L.
    Rights and realities : the judicial impact of the Canadian Charter
    of Rights and Freedoms on education, case law, and political
    jurisprudence / Jonathan L. Black-Branch.
        p.   cm.
    Includes bibliographical references.
    ISBN 1-85521-936-0 (hb)
    1. Educational law and legislation--Canada. 2. Civil rights-
-Canada. I. Title.
    KE3810.B58   1997
    344.71'07-dc21   97-7850
                                                               CIP

ISBN 1 85521 936 0

Printed and bound by Antony Rowe Ltd, Chippenham, Wiltshire

Contents

2 NEW DIRECTIONS IN EDUCATION 19

3 FUNDAMENTAL FREEDOMS 39

4   LEGAL RIGHTS

7 RIGHTS AND PRIVILEGES TO DENOMINATIONAL, SEPARATE AND DISSENTIENT SCHOOLS 145

Dedication

I dedicate this book to Dr. Mark Holmes (Professor Emeritus).

Preface

Since the enactment of the *Canadian Charter of Rights and Freedoms* in 1982, numerous books, monographs and articles have flooded the Canadian educational and legal communities. Educators and those interested in education seek to understand the *Charter* and how it affects day-to-day life in schools.

They hear talk about the "perceived" meaning of the *Charter*, the "intent" of the *Charter*. They hear talk of "changes". Traditional practices are "obsolete". New "must do" and "must not do" practices have since come into play. Educators are told to be "cautious"; these are "new" times, with new "rights" and "freedoms". But in the midst of this new rights culture, many remain ambivalent as to how the *Charter* actually affects life in Canadian schools. They know that until a clearer understanding of the *Charter* and its influence is reached, simply changing practices is not appropriate.

Although speculation remains, educators know one thing is for sure, contrary to tradition, where school-related decisions were left largely to educators, the school system is open, more than ever, to judicial scrutiny. Certainly there are, and will continue to be, increased threats of legal action as society becomes more and more litigious in the wake of a new rights consciousness which has evolved with the *Charter*. Proponents of change will use the *Charter* to promote their causes. Parents will insist on fair and equitable treatment. Further, children will demand more legal rights in relation to their personal freedoms.

The new role of the judiciary allows the opportunity to scrutinize the actions of educators, more so than in the past. This book illustrates the ways in which courts have already become involved. It provides a comprehensive understanding of how the *Charter* affects education by offering an overall synopsis of cases that have reached judicial fora.

The most important cases are presented in an abbreviated fashion to cut through difficult points of law and inform those interested in legal issues about the current state of Canadian education in respect to the *Charter*. Specifically, this book is intended to address the needs of three main groups of people: (1) administrators in schools and school boards (senior and middle level); (2) those interested in policy development within ministries and departments of education (and possibly other government departments); and, (3) students of education and law, be they in graduate law courses or in pre-service teacher education programmes. This is not to preclude others, however, as this text may serve as a valuable reference for teachers and academics alike, wishing to broaden their understanding of *Charter*-related activities as well as those involved in political lobby efforts relating to special interest causes.

The primary objective of this book is to clarify the effects and implications of the *Charter* on and for educational practice in Canada. The secondary objective is to put the impact of the *Charter* into a more general political framework. These objectives are achieved by highlighting the constitutional changes which have occurred in Canada with the entrenchment of the *Charter of Rights and Freedoms*. Specifically, the purpose of the first chapter is to provide a brief history of human rights developments, including discussion on the enactment of the United Nations Declaration of Human Rights, followed by the introduction of the *Canadian Bill of Rights* and the subsequent institution of the *Canadian Charter of Rights and Freedoms*.

Discussion in the second chapter focuses on what the *Charter* actually means, as constitutional law and how it may come to bear on education. Subsequent chapters three to eight focus on the main sections of the *Charter* and the education-related case law thereunder, namely: fundamental freedoms; legal rights; equality rights; minority language educational rights; denominational, separate and dissentient school rights; and, multiculturalism and the rights of aboriginal peoples.

The book concludes with chapter nine, an assessment of the comprehensive impact of the *Charter* on Canadian education, focusing on broader theoretical issues relating to the enforcement of the *Charter* and political jurisprudence. It expands on the secondary theme, which is woven throughout the book, that the entire policy area of education is political rather than judicial.[1]

Jonathan L. Black-Branch
Oxford, England

---

[1]   Please Note: The summary of the court directions and actions likely to be supported do not necessarily represent the author's own administrative philosophy but rather his interpretation of court-driven policy. Complete agreement on the rulings and the interpretation thereof is not to be expected. In addition, whilst this book covers most of the cases pertaining to education and the *Charter* it does not claim to be exhaustive. There may be important cases omitted from the discussion.

1 The Enactment of the Canadian Charter of Rights and Freedoms

Introduction

The *Canadian Charter of Rights and Freedoms*[1] is Canada's commitment to human rights. Unlike many human rights declarations, the *Charter*[2] is unique in at least two ways. Firstly, it addresses the specific needs of Canadians. That is to say, it is a document designed by Canadians for Canadians. Secondly, it is part of the Canadian Constitution. It is the supreme law of the land and no other laws can override the laws enlisted therein. The *Charter* cannot be changed or withdrawn simply with a majority vote in Parliament. There is an extensive procedure to which politicians must adhere in order to amend the Constitution. Difficulties which arise in that regard were clearly illustrated in the recent failed attempts to amend the Canadian Constitution through the enactment the *Meech Lake Accord* (1987) and later with the *Charlottetown Agreement* (1992). In other words, withdrawing the rights enlisted in the *Charter* would be very difficult.

The Parliamentary System of Governance

Canada did not always have a constitutionally entrenched bill of rights. In fact, this is a relatively new concept within the Canadian legal framework. The enactment of the *British North America Act 1867* (*B.N.A. Act*), now

---

[1]   The *Canadian Charter of Rights and Freedoms* may be referred to as the *Charter* or the *Canadian Charter* throughout this text.

[2]   See Appendix I for a complete copy of the *Canadian Charter*.

legally named the *Constitution Act 1867*, set into place a parliamentary system of government in Canada. This form of governance stems from the English system and is based on the concept of democratic majority rule. It allows for publicly elected officials to institute laws to govern the country. Over time, the parliamentary system evolved to become one in which representative government, based on universal suffrage, was essentially supreme, bound by the restrictions of the 1867 Act.

The Common Law System

The federal Government of Canada and all provinces follow a common law tradition, with the exception of the Province of Québec which follows a civil code. The role of judges in a common law system is to interpret laws and decide whether there has been compliance with existing legislation. In particular, "the common law approach is to scrutinize the judgements of previous cases and extract general principles to be applied to particular problems at hand" (Gall, 1990, p. 29). Specifically, court decisions are based on case precedent (former decisions by higher courts). Although, in principle, judges are bound by this doctrine of *stare decisis*, in practice they have the flexibility to stray from former judgements, thus introducing gradual change which reflects the societal context.[3]

The Civil Law System

The civil law system, on the other hand, is based on the notion that codified principles of law are supreme over individual cases and therefore judges need not abide by precedent. This is an adaptation of the Napoleonic or French Civil Code, which in turn, has its roots in Roman Law. Once again, the Province of Québec follows the civil code.

---

[3]   It should be noted that, in theory, under a common law system judges are primarily bound by statute law (i.e., legislation has priority over case law) except where otherwise stated under law.

The English Bill of Rights

At Confederation, Canada inherited the British tradition in regard to federal affairs and hence rights were not guaranteed under a constitutionally entrenched bill of rights.[4] The common law system in Canada did, however, guarantee individual rights and freedoms by tradition (e.g., *habeas corpus*).

   The year 1688 marked the Glorious Revolution in England whereby the people gained the right to limited control of governance. The Revolution was followed by the passing of the English Bill of Rights 1689. This Bill highlighted the respective powers of the monarchy and British Parliament. Aside from providing some guarantees against arbitrary legal penalties, historically speaking, the Bill was not a great achievement in the area of human rights. In modern times, the lack of formal recognition of human rights under the common law tradition was criticized by those who favoured more stringent guarantees such as would be provided under a codified system of constitutional law, such as in France and the United States.[5]

   Once again, Canada followed the British model and hence rights were not enshrined in a written constitution. Although there was growing pressure to modify the Canadian system by recognizing a code of human rights under law, no substantive changes were introduced in the early

---

[4]   Documents, such as *Magna Carta* (1215) and "tradition" (custom) are all part of England's Constitution and hence Canada's -- at least prior to the 1982 Constitution. Rights such as *habeas corpus* etc. were not guaranteed by written rights entrenched in constitutional bills of rights like in France and the United States.

[5]   The American Declaration of Independence states: "We hold these truths to be self-evident, that all men are created equal, that they are endowed by their creator with certain unalienable rights, that among these are life, liberty and the pursuit of happiness. That to secure these rights Governments are instituted among men deriving their just powers from the consent of the governed; that whenever any form of government becomes destructive of these ends, it is the right of the people to alter or abolish it and institute new government, laying its foundation on such principles and organizing its powers in such form, as to them shall seem most likely to effect their Safety and Happiness." Subsequent to this declaration came what is known today as the U.S. Bill of Rights.

   The French Declaration of the Rights of Man and of the Citizen 1789 states: "In the presence and under the auspices of the Supreme Being, the following rights of man and citizen: Men are born and remain free and equal in respect of rights. . . .The purpose of all civil associations is the preservation of the natural and imprescriptable rights of man. These rights are liberty, property and resistance to oppression."

years of Canadian nationhood. Issues concerning civil liberties and human rights first gained considerable world-wide attention after the Second World War.

Human Rights Developments in Canada

Many individual rights were withdrawn during World War II, in countries around the world.   There were many atrocities committed against particular groups and classes of peoples thus illustrating the precarious nature of human rights.   Lessons from this era, particularly in regard to Nazi Germany, reiterate that the power of government can be abused. Dominant world leaders sought to address such abuses.

The Atlantic Charter

The notion of protecting basic rights and fundamental freedoms was heightened in the early 1940s.   Discussion focused on issues involving political rights and civil liberties as questions regarding humanity and the dignity and worth of the individual took a world focus.   In 1941 Winston Churchill and Franklin Roosevelt spelled out four essential freedoms in what was called the Atlantic Charter.   These freedoms were: freedom of life;   freedom of religion;   freedom from want;   and, freedom from fear. But it was not until after World War II that commitment on an international level took hold.   At that point there was political resolve to have stronger monitoring and enforcement of minimum international standards of human rights.   From such dialogue came the establishment of the United Nations and the enactment of the Universal Declaration of Human Rights.

The United Nations and the Universal Declaration of Human Rights

The United Nations was formed with the intent of establishing an international commitment to protecting human rights on a global scale. On 10 December 1948, one of its first acts was the adoption of the Universal Declaration of Human Rights.   This declaration came about largely in response to governmental abuses of power and atrocities committed during World War II. It was considered "a significant milestone"[6] in protecting human rights.

This declaration provided a set of standards, a model or direction for countries to take. Moreover, it served as a precedent for individual countries to establish their own stand on human rights. The United Nations declaration states that "the inherent dignity" and "the equal and inalienable rights" of all people are "the foundation of freedom, justice and peace in the world". It repudiates "barbarous acts which have outraged the conscience of mankind" and encourages "the advent of a world in which human beings shall enjoy freedom of speech and belief and freedom from fear". Further, the declaration proclaims that "human rights should be protected by the rule of law", whilst promoting "the development of friendly relations between nations".

In short, the U.N. declaration is said to serve as an affirmation of faith in "fundamental human rights, in the dignity and worth of the human person and in the equal rights of men and women", whilst working to "promote the social progress and better standards of life". One of the United Nation's mandates is to promote "universal respect for and observance of human rights and fundamental freedoms". The enclosed preamble of the declaration expands upon its rational. Although it is somewhat lengthy, it is worth citing in its entirety.

THE UNIVERSAL DECLARATION OF HUMAN RIGHTS

Whereas recognition of the inherent dignity and of the equal and inalienable rights of all members of the human family is the foundation of freedom, justice and peace in the world,

Whereas disregard and contempt for human rights have resulted in barbarous acts which have outraged the conscience of mankind, and the advent of a world in which human beings shall enjoy freedom of speech and belief and freedom from fear and want has been proclaimed as the highest aspiration of the common people,

Whereas it is essential, if man is not to be compelled to have recourse, as a last resort, to rebellion against tyranny and

---

6   See van Dijk & van Hoof, 1992.

oppression, that human rights should be protected by the rule of law,

Whereas it is essential to promote the development of friendly relations between nations,

Whereas the peoples of the United Nations have in the Charter reaffirmed their faith in the fundamental human rights, in the dignity and worth of the human person and in the equal rights of men and women and have determined to promote the social progress and better standards of life in larger freedom,

Whereas member states have pledged themselves to achieve, in cooperation with the United Nations, the promotion of universal respect for and observance of human rights and fundamental freedoms,

Whereas a common understanding of these rights and freedoms is of the greatest importance for the full realisation of this pledge,

NOW THEREFORE THE GENERAL ASSEMBLY PROCLAIMS THIS UNIVERSAL DECLARATION OF HUMAN RIGHTS.

Canada was an active participant in the discussions in and around the establishment of the United Nations and the subsequent enactment of the Universal Declaration of Human Rights. Beyond this international treaty, some Canadians wanted these same guarantees entrenched in national laws.

The Canadian Commitment: Going Beyond the United Nations

Following the atrocities and obscene violations to individual dignity and security of the person which occurred during World War II, the need for protecting human rights was heightened. In Canada, the recognition of human rights such as its part in, and support of, the United Nation's Universal Declaration of Human Rights set the stage for deeper commitment to guaranteeing individual basic rights and fundamental freedoms. Many Canadians would not rest on the laurels of the United Nations declaration, however. They viewed the U.N. declaration as a symbolic document only,[7] stating that the British tradition of common law within Canada was an insufficient means of recognizing and upholding rights. They pushed for further recognition of human rights on the home front.

They argued that intentions to protect human rights and the dignity of the person can be overridden if they are not enshrined in special legislation, and indeed have special mechanisms in place for their monitoring and enforcement. This takes both political commitment and judicial support. For unless governments firstly embrace the notion of protecting the rights of its citizens, and secondly, enforce these same rights, they are not likely to be true rights but merely political platitudes recorded in impotent documents.

Canada's Human Rights Record

Politicians and interest groups sought to examine a means of incorporating human rights principles into the legal fabric of Canadian society. Traditionally, Canada's record with regards to human rights has been good. There are, however, some instances that blemish Canada's image regarding rights. Specifically, there have been occasions when Canada has denied certain rights to some classes of people, such as the treatment of the Chinese who came to Canada to build the Canadian Pacific Railroad; the treatment of Japanese-Canadians during World War II; and, the past and present treatment of aboriginal peoples. All the same, since World War II, Canada has been internationally regarded as a highly humanitarian nation, taking the role of "peace-keeper" during times of conflict and insurrection.

The Canadian Bill of Rights

On 10 August 1960, the *Canadian Bill of Rights* became law, under the leadership of Prime Minister John Diefenbaker. By that time Government commitment to human rights, in the form of legislation, had turned into a

---

[7]   Individuals cannot enforce these rights against a government-member of the United Nations.

long-standing debate amongst Canadians. In 1945, Co-operative Commonwealth Federation (C.C.F.) representative, Alistar Stuart, was the first member of the House of Commons to motion a Bill of Rights in Canada.[8]

In 1946 John Diefenbaker raised the issue of a federal Bill of Rights, stressing the need to protect Canadians with written legislation. Some Canadians opposed formal legislation vying their support for the common law tradition and the courts to protect Canadians. Diefenbaker continued the debate and shortly after his 1957 election as Prime Minister of Canada, he introduced Bill C-60, a Bill of Rights.

The *Bill of Rights* was passed in 1960. It put into writing basic rights that were said to have been formerly recognized by common law and guaranteed by tradition. Section 1 of the Bill states:

1. It is hereby recognized and declared that in Canada there have existed and shall continue to exist without discrimination by reason of race, national origin, colour, religion or sex, the following human rights and fundamental freedoms, namely,

   (a) the right of the individual to life, liberty, security of the person and enjoyment of property, and the right not to be deprived thereof except by due process of law;

   (b) the right of the individual to equality before the law and the protection of the law;

   (c) freedom of religion;

   (d) freedom of speech;

   (e) freedom of assembly and association; and

   (f) freedom of the press.

2. Every law of Canada shall, unless it is expressly declared by an Act of the Parliament of Canada that it shall operate notwithstanding the Canadian Bill of Rights, be so construed and applied as not to abrogate, abridge or infringe or to authorize the abrogation, abridgement or infringement of any of the rights or freedoms herein

---

[8]   In 1947, the C.C.F. Saskatchewan Government, was the first Canadian province to enact a Bill of Rights.

recognized and declared, and in particular, no law of Canada shall be construed or applied so as to

(a)   authorize or effect the arbitrary detention, imprisonment or exile of any person;

(b)   impose or authorize the imposition of cruel and unusual punishment;

(c)   deprive a person who has been arrested or detained
     (i)   of the right to be informed promptly of the reason for his arrest or detention;
     (ii)   of the right to retain and instruct counsel without delay, or
     (iii)   of the remedy by way of *habeas corpus* for the determination of the validity of his detention and for his release if the detention is not lawful;

(d)   authorize a court, tribunal, commission, board or other authority to compel a person to give evidence if he is denied counsel, protection against self incrimination or other constitutional safeguards;

(e)   deprive a person of the right to a fair hearing in accordance with the principles of fundamental justice for the determination of his rights and obligations;

(f)   deprive a person charged with a criminal offence of the right to be presumed innocent until proven guilty according to law in a fair and public hearing by an independent and impartial tribunal, or of the right to reasonable bail without just cause; or

(g)   deprive a person of the right to the assistance of an interpreter in any proceedings in which he is involved or in which he is a party or a witness, before a court, commission, board or other tribunal, if he does not understand or speak the language in which such proceedings are conducted.[9]

This Bill stood as a sense of pride and an achievement for many Canadians. It legally recognized Canada's commitment to human rights under federal legislation. But the strength of its legality was questionable.

---

[9]   Appendix II contains the complete wording of the *Canadian Bill of Rights*.

Constitutional critics argued that by virtue of its very nature, it was weak.

Limitations of the Canadian Bill of Rights

Essentially, there were fundamental weaknesses with the *Canadian Bill of Rights*. Firstly, Parliament could amend the *Bill* at any time. Secondly, other acts of Parliament could potentially ignore the primacy provision of the *Bill*. Thirdly, the *Bill of Rights* applied only to federal issues and not provincial ones. In addition, there were questions regarding the protection of newly acquired rights under the *Bill*, in what became known as the "frozen concepts" interpretation. Each of these are discussed in turn.

Amending the Bill of Rights

Being an act of Parliament, the House of Commons could amend the *Bill* at any time with a majority vote. As a result, this human rights legislation was not seen to be sufficiently out of the reach of elected politicians. These rights were hence perceived as being too political in nature. Critics questioned the utility of a commitment to human rights that could be amended or indeed withdrawn at any time. So if a Nazi-styled government were to take power they could easily suspend the rights of Canadians simply with a majority vote in Parliament.

Primacy Provision of the Bill of Rights

The *Bill of Rights* contained what is called a "primacy provision". Effectively, this requires that all other federal statutes must conform to the *Bill*. However, a similar provision could be placed in other federal statutes which would effectively allow them to overlook the provisions of the *Bill of Rights*. As a result, other Acts of Parliament could potentially deny the human rights provisions of the *Bill* once again calling into question the utility of a *Bill* that could be easily ignored or superseded.

Federal Jurisdiction of the Bill of Rights

According to section 91 of the *Constitution Act 1867,* an Act of Parliament (including the *Bill of Rights*) applies only to matters falling under federal jurisdiction. Section 91 states in its distribution of powers:

VI. DISTRIBUTION OF LEGISLATIVE POWERS
Powers of the Parliament

91. It shall be lawful for the Queen, by and with the Advice and Consent of the Senate and House of Commons, to make Laws for the Peace, Order, and Good Government of Canada, in relation to all Matters not coming within the Classes of Subjects by this Act assigned exclusively to the Legislatures of the Provinces; and for greater Certainty, but not so as to restrict the Generality of the foregoing Terms of this Section, it is hereby declared that (notwithstanding any of this Act) the exclusive Legislative Authority of the Parliament of Canada extends to all Matters coming within the Classes of Subjects next herein-after enumerated;

That is to say the federal *Bill of Rights* applies specifically to matters of federal jurisdiction and not to those under provincial jurisdictions such as education (as per section 93 of the Act). In relation to education, in the case of *Ward et al. and Board of the Blain Lake School Unit No. 57,* the applicant sought an order to quash a resolution passed by a local school board. The applicant argued that the provisions under the *Larger School Units Act* in Saskatchewan offended the *Bill of Rights.* The Court of the Queen's Bench ruled the *Canadian Bill of Rights* is not applicable to provincial legislation.

The Frozen Concepts Interpretation of Rights

The interpretation of the *Bill of Rights* is only applicable to rights which existed at the time the *Bill* was enacted. Newly acquired rights would not be protected by the *Bill*.   Tarnopolsky (as cited in Tarnopolsky and Beaudoin, 1982) calls this the "frozen concepts interpretation".[10]

Canadian Bill of Rights Summary

In short, the *Canadian Bill of Rights* served as a basic instrument to assist in interpreting federal statutes which protected legislative supremacy. Critics contend that the fact that it could be amended or rescinded in the House of Commons with a majority vote weakened the purpose of legally guaranteeing human rights.   The basic weaknesses as well as the hope of formally enshrining other rights into law led Canadian politicians and interest groups to seek further legal commitments.

Beyond the Canadian Bill of Rights

Pierre Elliot Trudeau, in particular, sought to guarantee rights and freedoms over all federal, and indeed provincial legislation.   It was long held that constitutional entrenchment would alleviate the weaknesses of the *Bill of Rights* whilst broadening the scope to include other rights and freedoms.   Many argued that the *Bill of Rights* maintained the *status quo* in that Parliament still had supremacy over human rights legislation. Trudeau held that entrenching rights and freedoms under a written constitution would curtail, if not eliminate, the powers of the federal and provincial legislatures over basic rights and fundamental freedoms. Throughout the 1960s, such thoughts gained prominence within political circles.

International Year of Human Rights

The year 1968 was declared by the General Assembly of the United Nations as *International Human Rights Year*. The United Nations staged international awareness campaigns focusing increasing world sensitivity to violations of human rights and individual freedoms. That same year,

---

10   This theory was never consistently applied, see *R. v. Drybones* [1970].

Prime Minister Lester B. Pearson, along with Pierre Elliot Trudeau, then Minister of Justice, argued for a Canadian Charter of Human Rights. Pearson stated:

> As Canada enters its second century of Confederation, Canadians could take no more meaningful step than to entrench firmly in our constitution those fundamental rights and liberties which we possess and cherish. A Canadian Charter of Human Rights would reflect and protect the high degree of freedom enjoyed by Canadians, and the unique bi-lingual character of the country. (Trudeau, 1968, p. 7)

Trudeau supported this position, adding: "A constitutional bill of rights in Canada would guarantee the fundamental freedoms of the individual from interference, whether federal or provincial. It would establish that all Canadians, in every part of Canada, have equal rights" (Trudeau, 1968, p. 11). Such a charter was seen to go beyond protecting "the unique bi-lingual character" of Canada. In reality, it would entrench the rights of a variety of Canadians and protect the so called Canadian "mosaic".

It was argued that the pluralistic nature of Canadian society calls for the protection of interests for all peoples. The varying interests within a multicultural state such as Canada, requires creative policy and governance with regard to guaranteeing individual rights and freedoms. Constitutional entrenchment of certain principles regarding human rights would effectively serve as a framework from which to guarantee a minimum standard of protection for all people. The need to promote an egalitarian society in face of pluralism continued to be heightened throughout the late 1960s and 1970s.

Patriating the Canadian Constitution

As Prime Minister of Canada, Trudeau later linked the notion of a Charter of Rights with that of patriating the Canadian Constitution. He wanted a written constitution with a codified system of rights (much like the French and American systems and unlike the British system of an unwritten constitution and no listed rights *per se*). Some Canadians agreed with the notion of a written and patriated constitution but not the inclusion of a charter; some agreed to having a charter but not the patriatation of the constitution; others did not want either. Some Canadians would accept the constitution if it included the existing *B.N.A. Act*, whilst others argued the *B.N.A. Act* would destroy the very purpose of patriating the constitution. Concomitant to these arguments were discussions of what would be included in this constitution and, in particular, which provisions would be in the Charter of Rights.

More and more, civil libertarians insisted that in a pluralistic society minorities must be protected against the potential tyranny of the majority.   Hence, the perceived need for constitutional protection increased as Canadian society continued to promote and celebrate its multicultural diversity. As a result, the need for the Charter increasingly moved to the forefront of people's minds. By the late 1970s the notion of the Charter had become a politically popular one, soon to be called "the people's *Charter*" (Clarkson & McCall, 1990).

The Debate Over the *Charter*

There was, and remains, considerable informed opinion, including that of many experts and legal scholars, that a charter like the *Canadian Charter* is inappropriate in a democracy.   Essentially, it passes the right to formulate policy to judges, who are "non-elected" officials. Inevitably, these officials may reflect the judgement and opinion of those who appoint them.[11]   In that regard, Cruickshank states that, "elected persons, not appointed judges, should be the final judges of how far freedoms, legal rights, and equality rights are permitted to go" (1986, p. 55).[12]

Conversely, the author would contend that the strength of a society lies in the protection of its weakest member. Such protection is more effectively achieved under human rights legislation which is constitutionally entrenched and enforced by an independent and impartial

---

[11]   There is much written on the experience in the United States regarding the politicization of the judiciary.

[12]   In the U.S., the President is elected and Supreme Court appointments are subject to review. The Canadian Prime Minister, in contrast, is simply the leader of the elected party. Appointed judges are not subject to review.

judiciary and not by elected politicians with overt and covert political agendas.

Debate regarding the *Charter of Rights and Freedoms* and the patriation of the Canadian Constitution raged on both sides of the Atlantic. In Canada, politicians and legal experts fought over wording, provinces fought over jurisdictions, and political activist groups fought over rights, leaving the Special Joint Committee of the Senate and the House of Commons inundated with varying opinions. Meanwhile, members of the British Houses of Parliament were faced with problems of their own. Interest groups and politicians lobbied to influence the manner by which the UK Parliament would handle Canada's request to enact the *Charter*.

The notion of constitutionally entrenched rights and freedoms was new to Britain. Canada was not merely exercising its independence, it was entering a new era that was unfamiliar territory to its mother country. Amid controversy and contention, in 1981 the Joint Senate and House Committee requested that Her Majesty the Queen put before the U.K. Parliament the *Canada Act 1982* (cited as 31 Elizabeth II).

In short, after much debate and strong opposition, fourteen years after the International Year of Human Rights, the *Canada Act* was signed, forever changing the nature of Canadian society by constitutionally entrenching the *Canadian Charter of Rights and Freedoms*.[13] The *Charter* was introduced as an important part of a new constitutional package know as the *Canada Act 1982*.

The *Canada Act*

The *Canada Act 1982*, was proclaimed in force 17 April 1982. This Act marked the patriation of the Canadian Constitution. Essentially, a constitution provides a basic framework from which the country operates. It creates the basic institutions of public authority. It defines the powers and privileges by which these public institutions operate. Moreover, it provides a mechanism for enacting laws to oversee the operation of the institutions.

With the enactment of the Constitution, Canada became completely independent from Britain (although for all intents and purposes

---

[13]   The *Charter* continues to recognize the *Canadian Bill of Rights*.

it had been independent for quite some time). The *Canada Act 1982* consists of four sections. Section one makes reference to Schedule B (the *Charter*) which in part is the main force of this text. Section two states that no Act of the U.K. Parliament shall apply to Canada after 17 April 1982. Section three provides that both the English and the French texts of the *Canada Act* are equally authoritative. Section four states that the name of the Act is the *Canada Act*.

The Constitution Act

Schedule B to the *Canada Act* is cited as the *Constitution Act 1982*. This Act incorporates the original agreement of Canadian Confederation, *British North America Act 1867*, now legally named the *Constitution Act 1867*, as well as other provisions. The institution of an Act of this nature contributes to a number of changes in Canadian Government. The *Constitution Act 1982*, however, continues to recognize Canada's eleven sovereign legislative bodies, specifically, the Parliament of Canada and the ten provincial legislatures. It also upholds most other laws and customs including the Governor General, and the provincial Lieutenant Governors.

The *Constitution Act 1982*, is divided into seven parts and includes a Schedule to the *Constitution Act 1982* for the *Modernisation of the Constitution*. Specifically, the *Constitution Act* is divided as follows: Part I of the *Constitution Act 1982* is the *Canadian Charter of Rights and Freedoms* (sections 1 to 34); Part II provides for *Rights of the Aboriginal Peoples of Canada* (section 35);   Part III contains provisions for *Equalisation and Regional Disparities* (section 36);   Part IV deals with *Constitutional Conference* (section 37);   Part V refers to the *Procedure for Amending Constitution of Canada* (sections 38 to 49);   Part VI provides for the Amendment to the *Constitution Act 1867*, formerly the *B.N.A. Act* (*British North America Act*) sections 50 and 51;   and, Part VII involves *General* concerns (sections 52 to 61).   In addition, the *Constitution Act 1982* includes the 1960 *Canadian Bill of Rights*.   Once again, the main thrust of this book focuses primarily on Part I of the *Constitution Act 1982*: the *Canadian Charter of Rights and Freedoms*.

The Charter

The *Charter* is the result of active participation of all levels of Government and many special interest groups. It is said to express the beliefs and attitudes that Canadians value about society. The Special Joint Committee of the Senate and House of Commons received over 1200 briefs expressing people's views on rights and freedoms. This information was instrumental during the drafting of the *Charter*. It assisted Canadian politicians in deciding the issues that were of most importance to Canadians.

> The *Canadian Charter of Rights and Freedoms* expresses beliefs that are at the heart of what Canadians most value about themselves. The document creates a momentum toward the realization of the hopes that it offers. It is a Canadian document that reflects the Canadian attitudes, approaches, respect for the individual and the values that have made the Canadian system of justice one of the most admirable, fair and decent in the history of mankind. (Laskin Greenspan, Dunlop and Rosenberg, 1982, p. 33-1)

The *Charter* was obviously a difficult document to write. The Joint Committee had a difficult task in taking all of the requests and shaping them into a document that was acceptable to most Canadians. It should be noted, however, that Premier René Lévesque of Québec did not sign the *Canada Act 1982*.[14]   Indeed, former Prime Minister Trudeau contends that constitutional negotiations between Québec and the federal Government, as well as other provinces have consistently been difficult.[15]

---

[14]   The Supreme Court of Canada later ruled that the Act was applicable to the Province of Québec.

[15]   Trudeau (*L'actualité 1er octobre*, 1992) argues that Québec Governments have continually rejected and blocked attempts to patriate the Canadian Constitution since 1927. He points out that agreements reached in 1964 and 1971 were rejected by Québec. But since the patriation of the Constitution in 1982 (which Premier Lévesque rejected), there have been political negotiations on the part of Québec to re-establish its place within Confederation. The failure to ratify the 1987 *Meech Lake Accord* left many Quebecers angry, and once again threatening to separate. But with time and some political coaxing, Premier Bourassa jumped back into the negotiating ring to bring Québec "back into"

Conclusion: Towards a Rights Conscious Society

For the first time in Canadian history, rights and freedoms take priority over all other laws, including the *Criminal Code of Canada*. This has inevitably changed Canadian society forever. As a result, there is little doubt that Canadians have become more rights conscious. In recent years people tend to speak more in terms of "rights", "freedoms" and personal "liberties". They are more likely to demand acceptable standards of care and treatment from their Federal and provincial Governments, be it in relation to matters of criminal due process or in the guarantee of everyday essential services. They will express certain expectations as their fundamental rights as citizens of the state.

Indeed, there is an ever-deepening "rights culture" throughout Canada as more and more individuals assert their rights. Whilst many of these assertions are personal desires and not rights *per se* under the *Charter*, others are duly recognized as having the strength of constitutional law. As a result, the *Charter* is being used as a vehicle by which individuals affect change within public sector institutions. The legal and socio-political implications of such change, in regard to education and its administration, are the focus of this book.

Canada, with the hopes of once and for all establishing Québec as a "legally recognized" distinct society within Canada.

After difficult negotiations and a nasty referendum campaign, in 1992 the Canadian electorate said "No" to the *Charlottetown Agreement*. Since this time there has been another referendum whereby the Québécois rejected the notion of a separation, albeit by a narrow margin. Nevertheless, the future of Québec remains uncertain as Quebecers are left to decide, once again, whether to become really distinct and actually separate from Canada, or they may gain their cherished status as a "distinct society" with some form of re-negotiated sovereignty association.

2 New Directions in Education

Introduction

Constitutional law, lawyers and courts may at first seem far removed from day-to-day life in Canadian schools. But in reality, the legal principles entrenched in the *Charter of Rights and Freedoms*[1] carry with them many legal repercussions for most school systems throughout Canada. In fact, legal implications will inevitably impinge on educational policy and practice at every level, including: governance, administration and teaching. Hence, the *Charter* affects the lives of administrators, teachers, students and parents alike.

Signing the *Charter* into Law

On 17 April 1982, Queen Elizabeth II and Prime Minister Pierre Elliot Trudeau signed into law the *Canada Act 1982*, forever changing Canadian tradition. The Act includes the *Canadian Charter of Rights and Freedoms*. The *Charter* guarantees a variety of basic rights and fundamental freedoms under constitutional law. These laws are superior to all federal and provincial statutes. They form the "supreme law of the land", taking precedence over all Government actions.

Application of the *Charter*

Section 32(1) of the *Charter* states that the Government of Canada, and

---

[1] Appendix I contains a complete copy of the *Canadian Charter*. See also Table 1.1, presented later in this chapter, for a comprehensive breakdown of the main features of the *Charter* applicable within the educational context.

the Governments of each province, must respect the rights and freedoms enlisted in the *Charter*. Specifically, the *Charter* states:

> *Application of Charter*
> 32(1)   This Charter applies
>
> (a)   to the Parliament and government of Canada in respect of all matters within the authority of Parliament including all matters relating to the Yukon Territory and Northwest Territories; and
>
> (b)   to the legislature and government of each province in respect of all matters within the authority of the legislature of each province.

To the extent that schools and school systems operate under Government legislation, they too are considered government. In other words, the *Charter* is designed to protect individuals from the power of wrongs by the state. Schools act as agents of the state[2] and are not permitted to proceed in any manner which violates *Charter* provisions.[3] Schools and school systems must fall within *Charter* guidelines, hence educators must amend policies and reassess practices or face litigation.

The Traditional Exclusivity of Education

Prior to the enactment of the *Charter*, court proceedings were reserved mainly for issues dealing with the interpretation of statutes. Judicial intervention was largely restricted to compliance with legislation governing education found in the various provincial Education Acts, and the regulations thereunder.[4] The day-to-day concerns of school life were

---

2   Please note that private schools are exempt from many provisions of the *Charter*.

3   Subject, of course, to some important exceptions which are discussed throughout this chapter.

4   Education is a provincial responsibility pursuant to section 93 of the *Constitution Act 1867* (formerly called the *B.N.A. Act*). See Chapter seven for more discussion on this point.

seldom held to judicial scrutiny.

Educators held a wide scope of autonomy regarding decision-making for the safety, security and general well-being of the school community.   This was particularly true when dealing with issues of student discipline, including daily routines.[5]   Other than in extreme circumstances, courts were reluctant to deal with educational issues.   In essence, school administrators traditionally enjoyed almost exclusive control over schools and school systems.[6]

Courts Seizing A Wider Role in Education

With the advent of the *Charter* there comes a change to this long-standing tradition.   Human rights laws enshrined in the *Charter* are superior to all federal and provincial statutes, including education statutes.   Moreover, the *Charter* has changed the role of the Canadian judiciary.   Judges no longer simply interpret law to determine wrongdoings; they can judge the laws themselves.

The *Charter* grants judges the power to scrutinize laws to ensure compliance with these rights.   Chief Justice Antonio Lamer, in an interview commemorating the tenth anniversary of the *Charter of Rights and Freedoms* (in 1992) stated that there is no doubt that the courts have seized a wider role in scrutinizing laws.   In the article "How the *Charter* changes justice" Chief Justice Lamer stated "not only to this court [the Supreme Court of Canada], but all courts and judges, the *Charter* has changed our job descriptions . . . . with the *Charter* we are commanded

---

5   Two examples of court cases which illustrate this traditional notion of the courts leaving matters concerning the disciplining of students to the discretion of school authorities are the cases of *McIntyre v. The Public School Trustees of Section Eight in the Township of Blanchard et al.* (1886) and *Re Ward and Board of Blaine Lake School* (1971).   Both these cases perfectly illustrate "judicial deference" to the discretion of school administrators. *McIntyre* and *Ward* are but two examples of this pre-*Charter* tradition of school administrative discretion deferred by Canadian courts to school officials.   Both of these cases are discussed further in Chapter three, Legal Rights.

6   At least as far as judicial interpretation is concerned.   There was, and still is, significant legislative control.

. . . to sometimes judge the laws themselves" (*Globe & Mail*, 17 April, 1992).[7]

Courts now have the authority to strike down laws (including policies and practices) which violate the provisions in the *Charter*. As a result, the entrenchment of basic rights and fundamental freedoms, concomitant with this change in the role of the judiciary mandates change within schools and school systems. Many legal implications will follow.

Charter Issues Not Easily Defined

There is no doubt that the *Charter* has encroached, and will continue to encroach, on all levels of educational decision-making. The notion of changing educational practices to accommodate the provisions in the *Charter* may not be so clear cut, however. Issues concerning the *Charter* are neither easily defined nor understood. Educational systems are different in each province and, in some instances, different within individual provinces themselves. Regulations governing education vary and *Charter* laws have potentially differing effects on them.

In addition, the *Charter* is subject to legal interpretation. Until an understanding of the *Charter* is reached, it may be premature to make assumptions regarding "necessary" changes to traditional practices within the educational sector. As a result, there is a degree of uncertainty that makes it difficult for educators to speculate on the actual, or indeed the intended, meaning of the *Charter*.

Charter Ambiguity and Open-Endedness

By virtue of both its wording as well as its place within the constitutional framework, the *Charter of Rights and Freedoms* is a complex legal document. Canada is guided by the *Canada Act 1982*. This Act consists of the *Constitution Act 1867* and the *Constitution Act 1982*. Once again the *Charter of Rights and Freedoms* is a component of the *Constitution Act 1982*. Constitutional experts readily acknowledge that within this framework, the meaning and intent of the provisions in the *Charter* may

---

7   For further reading on the *Charter*, see also: "Revolutionary-change agent", [Toronto] *Globe and Mail*, (1992, 25 November).

not be as clearly defined as one would hope. The wording is often open-ended and subject to legal and judicial interpretation.

The *Charter* and Political Agendas

Legal experts agree that interpretations of provisions within the *Charter* will be shaped largely by political agendas. So different individuals or groups will attempt to use the *Charter* to the advantage of their particular cause. That is, they will advance interpretations of the *Charter* in a manner which best suits their needs.

The *Charter* and Competing Interests

In addition, some provisions within the *Charter*, and the *Canada Act* in general, have apparently competing interests. Legal wording within the *Constitution Acts* (1867 and 1982) may seem to work toward different ends. Examples of such competing interests will be provided later in this chapter.

Charter Rights Are Not Absolute

Furthermore, a number of clauses in the *Charter* itself are designed to actually limit the provisions enlisted therein, hence these rights and freedoms are not absolute. Firstly, all guarantees are subject to the reasonableness test. Secondly, some rights and freedoms may be temporarily withdrawn (to be discussed later in this chapter). In sum, basic rights and fundamental freedoms enshrined in the *Charter* are not absolute and therefore are not easily defined. In other words, the "supreme law of the land" may not be sacrosanct.

The *Charter* within an Educational Context

As per the above discussion, at least four issues must be taken into account when examining rights and freedoms within an educational context.[8] These are: (1) the limitations clause in the *Charter*;   (2) the notwithstanding clause (*non-obstanante*) in the *Charter*;   (3) variations in legal interpretations of individual provisions in the *Charter*;   and, (4) competing interests of some of the provisions in the *Charter* and the *Canada Act* as a whole.   Each of these topics is discussed in turn, in regard to the educational context.

The Limitations Clause

Rights and freedoms in the *Charter* have justifiable limits. In other words, they are not absolute. Subject to judicial scrutiny, limitations may be placed on rights and freedoms in order to promote a broader social "good" within the Canadian community. Such limitations are aimed at protecting the overall rights and freedoms of Canadians as a collective. That is to say, one's rights are only protected to a certain point and then may be withdrawn or limited. Section 1 of the *Charter* states:

> The Canadian Charter of Rights and Freedoms guarantees the rights and freedoms set out in it subject only to such reasonable limits prescribed by law as can be demonstrably justified in a free and democratic society.

This limitations clause was deemed necessary by politicians at the time of enacting the *Charter* in order to curtail abuses of rights and freedoms by extremist individuals using their rights to work against the perceived "good" of society. Its purpose is to protect the community against potentially divisive and negative consequences which stem from the absolute exercise of rights and freedoms. For example, a person promoting hatred against a certain class of people may ultimately be denied his or her freedom of speech. As a result, freedom of speech is not absolute, it does have limits.[9]

---

[8] Those pertaining to private schools are substantially different.

[9] Actual examples of cases dealing with issues of freedom of expression will be discussed in the cases of *Keegstra* and *Ross* presented later in this book.

Reasonable Limits

Reasonable limits may be placed on the rights and freedoms enshrined in the *Charter*. The phrase "only to such reasonable limits" indicates that limits may be imposed on *Charter* guarantees, so long as they are "reasonable". Thus, judges can limit rights. Essentially, when making rulings, a court first determines whether a *Charter* right has been violated. If the answer is "yes", then the court must decide whether the violation can be justified under section 1 of the *Charter* [this procedure is known as the Oakes test and is described below]. As a result, many people, including Judge Zuker (1988), claim that section 1 may well be the "most important section" in the *Charter*.

The function of this clause is to mute the absolute character of the stated rights. Interestingly, the authority to determine whether a right should apply in a given circumstance lies with the courts and not with Parliament (section 33, to be discussed later in this chapter, excepted). Thus the courts may determine that although a given right has been abrogated, such an abrogation is reasonable and justified within the circumstances. So in some instances, subject to the discretion of the judiciary, schools and school systems can limit freedoms within the educational context.

Reasonable Limits Prescribed by Law

Such limitations, however, must adhere to certain guidelines. For example, limits to individual rights can only be imposed or "prescribed by law". That is to say, limits to individual rights and freedoms in schools must have the force of law. Violative policies and practices (be they administrative directives, practices, or decisions) that do not have the status of "law" cannot operate as limitations on the *Charter* rights and freedoms.

In early rulings under the *Charter* such as the case of *Québec Association of Protestant School Boards v. Attorney-General of Québec* [1984], and *Re: Germany and Rauca* (1983), the courts were reluctant to define the scope of section 1. In 1986, the Supreme Court of Canada gave its ruling concerning the application and interpretation of section 1 in what has become known as the Oakes Test.

The Oakes Test

In *R. v. Oakes* the Supreme Court definitively spelled out the nature of the limitations clause. The Oakes Test provides a two-step analysis to determine whether a law is a "reasonable limit" and is "demonstrably justified". In the decision Chief Justice Dickson of the Supreme Court of Canada stated:

> It is important to observe at the outset that section 1 has two functions: first, it constitutionally guarantees the rights and freedoms set out in the provisions which follow; and, second, it states explicitly the exclusive justificatory criteria (outside of section 33 of the Constitution Act, 1982) against which limitations on those rights and freedoms must be measured. (*R. v. Oakes* [1986] 2 S.C.R. 713)

The *Oakes* decision provided the means by which future courts would determine reasonable limits. Applying this test in *R. v. Edwards Books and Art Ltd.*, Chief Justice Dickson explains the procedure. He stated:

> Two requirements must be satisfied to establish that a limit is reasonable and demonstrably justified in a free and democratic society. First, the legislative objective which the limitation is designed to promote must be of sufficient importance to warrant overriding a constitutional right. It must bear on a "pressing and substantial concern". Second, the means chosen to attain those objectives must be proportional or appropriate to the ends. The proportionality requirement, in turn, normally has three aspects: the limiting measure must be carefully designed, or rationally connected, to the objective; they must impair the right as little as possible; and their effects must not so severely trench on individual or group rights that the legislative objective, albeit important, is nevertheless outweighed by the abridgement of rights. (*R. v. Edwards Books and Art Ltd.* (1986) 28 C.R.R. 1 at 40-41)

The Political Role of the Judiciary

In short, this judicially devised test encourages courts to assume more of a political role than one that is purely judicial in nature. As a result, the Canadian judiciary can make rulings which limit actions (freedoms) if they are seen as reasonable and justified, especially in the sense of being for the "greater good" of Canadian society. In certain circumstances, the rights of some individuals may take priority over the rights of others. For example, it has been accepted by the Supreme Court of Canada that people promoting hate literature toward certain groups (such as the Alberta school teacher, James Keegstra)[10] can be denied their freedom of expression in that regard. Critics warn that section 1 provides a powerful political tool for the courts whereby they can use their judicial discretion to make political value judgements.[11]

The Notwithstanding Clause

Another limitation to rights and freedoms lies in section 33, the "notwithstanding clause" (*non-obstanante*). Section 33 is a special *Charter* provision that enables elected politicians, in either the federal Parliament or the provincial legislatures, to legally limit rights and freedoms under section 2 and sections 7 to 15 of the *Charter*.

Once again, section 2 guarantees fundamental freedoms such as: religion, belief, expression, and association. Sections 7 to 14 are legal rights which address issues such as: life, liberty and security of person, search and seizure, detention, and proceedings in criminal and penal matters. Section 15 addresses issues of equality rights. Each of these is discussed further in their respective chapters: three, four and five.

Undoubtedly, many of these rights and freedoms are of particular importance in the educational sector hence section 33 is an important

---

[10]   The *Keegstra* (1990) case will be discussed in Chapter three.

[11]   The politicization of the courts is a secondary theme of this book. The author highlights cases where the courts are using their position to promote a dominant ideology within the educational policy arena, both by using section 1 and in their interpretation of rights generally. The dominant ideology is one of maintaining the political *status quo* over a purely interpretative stance on human rights issues.

clause to bear in mind whilst understanding the precarious nature of rights and freedoms guaranteed in the *Charter*. Section 33 states:

33(1)	Parliament or the legislature of a province may expressly declare in an Act of Parliament or of the legislature, as the case may be, that the Act or a provision thereof shall operate notwithstanding a provision included in section 2 or sections 7 to 15 of this Charter.
33(2)	An Act or provision of an Act in respect of which a declaration made this section is in effect shall have such operation as it would have but for the provision of this Charter referred to in the declaration.
33(3)	A declaration made under subsection (1) shall cease to have effect five years after it comes into force or on such earlier date as may be specified in the declaration.
33(4)	Parliament or the legislature of a province may re-act a declaration made under subsection (1).
33(5)	Subsection (3) applies in respect of a re-enactment made under subsection (4).

Sovereignty of Parliament

In other words, the over-ride power of section 33 allows for parliamentary supremacy over these rights and freedoms, if invoked. This means that Parliament (in regard to federal matters) and the legislatures (in regard to those within provincial jurisdictions) are ultimately sovereign over these affairs. Sovereignty of Parliament means that, "the legislative competence of Parliament is unlimited. No court . . . can question its power to enact any law it pleases" (Oxford Concise Dictionary of Law, 1990).[12]

So provincial legislators could feasibly use the notwithstanding clause in reference to education statutes to achieve a purpose that may

---

[12]   The courts cannot question the laws that Parliament enact in this regard. They can, however, examine whether Parliament had the power to enact such laws. If Parliament acted *ultra vires* (outside its powers) then the courts can issue a ruling in that regard.

actually violate the above stated legal and equality rights or fundamental freedoms. In other words, a legislature could deny individual freedoms to meet certain ends, such as social, linguistic or political agendas. It would, however, have to state the specific intent upfront and answer to the electorate as to why they want to deny such liberties.

So, as a matter of illustration, a provincial government could choose to actively promote Christianity in non-denominational public schools, by voting to limit freedom of religion under the limitations clause. This limit would be valid for a period of five years and could be reinstated for another five with a majority vote in the legislature.

Use of the Notwithstanding Clause

There have been four instances where governments have either invoked or have attempted to invoke the notwithstanding clause under the *Charter*. Firstly, the Government of Québec enacted a law providing that all Québec laws "shall operate notwithstanding the provisions of section 2 and sections 7 to 15". This legislation, however, was struck down by the Québec Court of Appeal stating the use of this clause had to be within the specific context of a particular law.

It should be noted however, that including cultural rights and "distinct society" status for the Province of Québec in the *Charter*, as was proposed in the *Charlottetown Agreement* (1992), would inadvertently strengthen the Québec Government's position in the future.[13] Courts may be willing to allow more leeway in that regard if they have what the author would call "enhanced rights" enshrined in the *Charter*.[14] Courts

---

[13]   Distinct Society has been politically agreed upon in principle twice by former Prime Minister Mulroney and the ten premiers but has never been ratified because of subsequent opposition. The first time was under the *Meech Lake Accord* (1987). The second time was under the *Charlottetown Agreement* (1992) which was sent to a national public referendum involving nine of the ten provinces and the two territories. The Province of Québec held a provincial referendum, regarding the same issues, and the same question, on the same day as the national vote. Some contend that part of the opposition to the Charlottetown Agreement is attributed in some provinces to opposition to Québec's "special" treatment.

[14]   Trudeau feels that all provinces, including Québec, were distinct in their own way upon entering Confederation. "Mais cette constitution a également donné naissance à

may allow for laws aimed at advancing the special interests of this linguistic group of people. The author would contend that the Québécois already enjoy élitist minority status within Canada as a whole. That is their linguistic interests are well-entrenched within the Constitution and are protected in the same form as that of a majority group.[15]

Secondly, the Government of Alberta threatened to use this clause when public servants challenged (in court) a law prohibiting them to strike. The Government said if it lost the case it would invoke section 33 to maintain the law. The Government won the case and hence did not have to invoke section 33.

Thirdly, following the Alberta decision, the Government of Saskatchewan used section 33 to immunize its labour laws from section 2 of the *Charter*.

Fourthly, the Québec Government instituted section 33 to counteract the court decision in the *Ford v. Attorney General of Québec* [1988] case concerning the unconstitutionality of Québec's language laws. (It should be noted that Québec routinely uses a similar opting out provision with respect to its own human rights legislation.)

Notwithstanding Clause: Politically Contentious

Although the notwithstanding clause has indeed been used in the past it is considered a politically contentious issue. That is to say, it must be enacted under law, which requires a majority vote in the House of Commons or the provincial legislature. As a result, there is usually debate in relation to the issue at hand and hence media hype. Given that, the use of this clause to deny or to limit rights and freedoms is not particularly popular with politicians. Prime Ministers to date, for example, have not used it regarding federal legislation and, in fact, encourage provincial legislatures to follow their example. Nevertheless,

neuf autres provinces, toutes distinctes les une des autres en vertu de leurs frontières propres, de leur composantes ethniques, de leurs lois et partant de leurs cultures. (En effet, une société ne saurait être distincte par rapport à une autre sans que cette autre ne soit distincte par rapport à elle)" (L'actualité, 1er octobre, 1992, p. IV).

[15]   The position of "privilege" comes only when legislatures (federal or provincial) and the courts freeze the existing rights, or in the case of the French actually serve to expand them, whilst refusing to grant equivalent rights to other minorities.

since education falls within the jurisdiction of the provinces and they seem willing to use the notwithstanding clause, it may well be that they decide to use it to meet politically "desirable ends" within the educational sector, or at least the threat of its use to meet an end.

The Legal Interpretation of the *Charter*

Aside from the notwithstanding clause and the reasonable limits clause, many of the provisions within the *Charter* are open-ended and subject to legal interpretation. That is to say, different people offer varying opinions regarding the meaning and the intent of the *Charter*. For example, section 15, the equality rights provision, (to be discussed in greater depth in Chapter Five) is open-ended and subject to legal and judicial interpretation. The wording of section 15(1), guaranteeing equality is broad in scope and not clear in its definition of equality. Legal scholars offer varying opinions regarding the intent of this provision. Ultimately, the courts are left to make a decision.

Furthermore, section 28 specifies that the rights and freedoms in the *Charter* are "guaranteed equally to male and female persons". But there is a noted contradiction regarding equality for both gender groups because section 15(2), the affirmative action clause (which takes precedence over section 15(1) and permits any "program or activity that has as its object the amelioration of conditions of disadvantaged individuals or groups"), potentially gives primacy to one gender or one group of people over another. This clearly sends the message that "equality", as guaranteed by the *Charter*, is not simply equal treatment of all persons (once again this will be discussed in greater depth in Chapter five, Equality Rights).

Uniqueness and Variations in School Systems

Educators will ultimately turn to the courts to interpret the *Charter* in hopes of clarifying the many ambiguities. Whilst some judicial interpretations will apply broadly to all schools and school systems, others may be situational. Each school system is unique, having an infrastructure consisting of a number of provincially enacted laws with regulations emanating from those laws. In addition, there are school board policies, rules, and regulations, as well as the school's own rules and policies. Further, collective agreements are shaped between employees -- notably teachers -- and the employer, which may be the province itself or a local school board acting under the authority of the province.[16]

Boards of education typically act according to three types of regulatory guides including: "(1) prescriptions, which are specifications of what a board *must do*; (2) prohibitions, which are specifications of what a board *must not do*; and (3) permissions, specified and unspecified, of what a board *may do*, which set the scope of a board's freedom to govern" (Downey, 1988, p. 8). These statutory and regulatory guidelines are set by provincial governments and are further defined by individual boards of education. MacKay (1984) uses the illustration that "often the [provincial] statute is only the skeleton of a legal scheme; the regulations, rules, and policies are the flesh" (p. 4).

The influence of these broad sets of rules has been immensely variable, from province to province, from school system to school system, and from school to school over time. Hence, legal interpretation of the *Charter* may apply differently as per individual province, individual school board, or even within individual schools themselves. In essence, it is difficult to apply a broad set of federal principles under the *Charter* to provinces which vary both amongst one another and indeed within themselves.

Competing Interests

Furthermore, some provisions enlisted in the *Charter* appear to compete with other *Charter* rights and specific components of the *Constitution Act 1867*. Section 29, for example, is technically at odds with sections 2 and 15, thus causing competing interests within the *Charter* itself.

Specifically, section 29 reaffirms the rights of denominational, separate and dissentient schools, as spelled out under section 93 of the *Constitution Act 1867*. Both sections, however, may be construed as inconsistent with section 2 which guarantees freedom of conscience and

---

[16]   For a more comprehensive overview of Canadian school systems, refer to *Teachers' Working Conditions in Canada* (Black-Branch, 1991).

religion, thought, belief, opinion, and expression. In addition, it may be said to be inconsistent with section 15 dealing with equality rights. This raises the issue of how the *Charter* provides that everybody enjoys freedom of religion and equality when another section upholds what some groups would call "discriminatory" notions of special religious schooling, especially where such notions vary widely from province to province.[17]

Summary: The Ambiguity of the *Charter* Within the Educational Context

In summary, the complexity of the *Charter* as a legal document often lends itself to problems of interpretation. Justifiable limits can be placed on rights and freedoms. Governments can retain supremacy over certain rights. The *Charter* is open-ended and ambiguous, sometimes comprising provisions that may appear to be at odds with others. Whilst uncertainty may prevail in that light, one thing is certain, the notion of judicial intervention in educational matters is a growing trend in post-*Charter* Canada. Evidently, the results of these challenges will invariably depend on a number of factors, not least of which is the nature of the challenge itself. Understanding the complexities of the *Charter* is a first step toward understanding the judicial decision-making processes involved in deciding education-related issues thereunder.

Types of Court Challenges

Given that educators act as agents of the state, individuals or groups who allege their rights have been violated by the state (either by educators acting within a school capacity or by the laws governing education) can make application to the courts for a ruling on the issues at hand. In particular, three types of applications can be filed under the *Charter*, namely: (1) the request for a remedy by a party whose rights have been violated; (2) the request to exclude evidence that was obtained by violating *Charter* rights; or (3) a request to strike down legislation that violates *Charter* rights.

---

17   Issues relating to religious schools are discussed in Chapter seven of this book.

The Request for a Remedy

The first type, requesting a remedy, is guaranteed under section 24(1) of the *Charter*. Specifically, this section states that "anyone whose rights or freedoms have been infringed or denied may apply to a court of competent jurisdiction to obtain such remedy as the court considers appropriate and just in the circumstances". A remedy may be in the form of damages, an injunction, a decree of specific performance or a declaration by the court.

The Request to Exclude Evidence

The second type is an application for the court to exclude evidence that was obtained in a manner which was unconstitutional. Under section 24(2), an individual can apply to a court to exclude the use of evidence that was "obtained in a manner that infringed or denied" the rights of the accused. Such a judicial decision would be based on the fact that the admission of such evidence in proceedings against an individual "would bring the administration of justice into disrepute". In short, such evidence would be excluded from the hearing because it was obtained illegally.

The Request to Strike Down Legislation

The third kind of application is a request to strike down government legislation. Section 52(1) of the *Constitution Act 1982*, states: "The *Constitution* of Canada is the supreme law of the land, and any law that is inconsistent with the provisions of the *Constitution* is, to the extent of the inconsistency, of no force or effect". Laws that violate rights and freedoms are subject to judicial scrutiny.

Summary: A New Rights Era

Whilst Canadians live in a new era with constitutionally entrenched rights and freedoms with a new role behaviour for judges, there is little doubt that educators must be more concerned about their practices. But to suggest changing education as a result of the mere existence of the *Charter* reflects either a simplistic, or a wishful, understanding of the nature and the meaning of the *Charter*. As discussed throughout this chapter, interpreting the *Charter* is complex. Limitations may be placed on rights and there appear to be many competing interests within the Constitution as a whole. Whilst it is essential to reassess existing policies and current practices, it is best to do so from the perspective of an informed, critical thinker.

The intent of this book is to present a deeper understanding of the legal status of the *Charter*. Each chapter highlights important sections of the *Charter*, focusing on specific *Charter* provisions and case law thereunder. Discussion focuses on education-related cases which have been heard in the various provinces. This compilation of *Charter* cases and judicial rulings endeavours to clarify some of the ambiguity regarding the *Charter* and how it relates to schools and school systems throughout Canada. Also presented are practical applications for those with a stake in education and how the courts have become dominant players in the political process.

Table 1:   Sections of the *Canadian Charter of Rights and Freedoms* Most Applicable Within the Educational Context.[18]

The *Charter*

Section 1:   **Guarantee of Rights and Freedoms. (Limitations Clause)**

Section 2:   **Fundamental Freedoms: Freedom of conscience, religion, thought, belief, opinion and expression, assembly, and association.**

Section 7:   **The right to life, liberty and security of person. (Due Process)**

Section 8:   **The right against unreasonable search or seizure.**

Section 9:   **The right not to be arbitrarily detained or imprisoned.**

Section 10:   ***inter alia* The right to be informed promptly of the reasons for arrest or detention and the right to counsel without delay and to be informed of that right.**

Section 11:   ***inter alia*   The right to be informed without unreasonable delay of the specific offence to which one is charged and the right to be presumed innocent until proven guilty according to law in a fair and public hearing by an independent and impartial tribunal.**

Section 12:   **The right not to be subjected to any cruel and unusual treatment or punishment.**

Section 13:   **The right against self-incrimination.**

---

18   Source: This table serves as the author's abbreviated version of the *Canadian Charter of Rights and Freedoms* for educators.

Section 14:   The right to the assistance of an interpreter.

Section 15:   Equality Rights: 15(1) The right to be equal before and under the law; and the right to the equal protection and equal benefit of the law without discrimination. 15(2) Affirmative Action. (Positive Discrimination)

Sections 16 to 22:   Official Languages of Canada: English and French are the official languages of Canada and have equality of status and equal rights and privileges.

Section 23:   Minority Language Education Rights: The right of the English or French linguistic minority population of a province to have their children receive primary and secondary school instruction in the minority language of that province.

Section 24:   Enforcement of the Charter.

Section 25:   The rights of the Aboriginal Peoples of Canada.

Section 27:   The preservation and enhancement of the multicultural heritage of Canadians.

Section 28:   Equality of male and female persons.

Section 29:   The rights and privileges accorded to denominational, separate or dissentient schools.

Section 33:   The notwithstanding clause. (Affecting section 2 and sections 7 to 15)

The *Constitution Act* 1982

Section 52:   Laws that are inconsistent with the provisions of the Canadian Constitution are of no force or effect.

3 Fundamental Freedoms

Introduction

The 1982 enactment of the *Canadian Charter of Rights and Freedoms* forever changed the nature of Canadian society. For the first time in history, Canadians are guaranteed fundamental freedoms under constitutional law. Civil liberties such as the freedom of religion and freedom of expression have become the "supreme law of the land". As a result, educational policy or practice that discriminates against individuals on the basis of fundamental beliefs or preferences now come under scrutiny as an alleged violation of the *Charter*. Those feeling discriminated against can seek recourse in the courts.

Fundamental Freedoms

Fundamental freedoms guarantee personal freedoms both in private life as well as in public life, i.e., public institutions such as schools. The *Charter* specifically states:

2.   Everyone has the following fundamental freedoms:

(a)   freedom of conscience and religion;
(b)   freedom of thought, belief, opinion and expression, including freedom of the press and other media of communication;
(c)   freedom of peaceful assembly; and
(d)   freedom of association.

Fundamental Freedoms and Education

Disputes over religious observances and alleged Christian indoctrination are high on the list of *Charter* decisions. Specifically, the main cases discussed in this chapter involve issues of fundamental freedoms regarding: religious freedoms, including the reading of scriptures and the recitation of the Lord's Prayer; disputes over religious curricula; mandatory school enrolment and compulsory attendance; and, mandatory membership in a teachers' federation. Other cases involve freedom of expression and freedom of speech.

Reading Scriptures and Reciting the Lord's Prayer

Sections of the Ontario *Education Act* and the British Columbia *School Act*, regarding the compulsory reading of scriptures and the recitation of the Lord's Prayer, as opening or closing ceremonies to the school day, have been struck down under the *Charter*. The cases of *Zylberberg et al. v. Director of Education of the Sudbury Board of Education* (1988) and *Russow et al. v. Attorney General of British Columbia* (1989) both related to the reading of scriptures and the recitation of the Lord's Prayer in public schools. These practices were judged to contravene section 2(a), freedom of conscience and religion. In both of these cases portions of the respective Acts were judged as unconstitutional, being of "no force or effect", pursuant to section 52 of the *Constitution Act 1982*.

Religious Readings and Prayer in Ontario

In the *Zylberberg* case, the Ontario Court of Appeal stated that the religious exercises prescribed under section 50 of the Ontario *Education Act* (and section 28 of Regulation 262) contravened the plaintiff's right to religious freedom. Zylberberg argued that the requirement for the reading of scriptures and the repeating of the Lord's Prayer (or other scriptures or prayers in public schools) placed psychological pressure on non-Christian children to conform to Christian observances. Although the non-Christian students were permitted to abstain from Christian religious exercises, the plaintiffs argued that their children were thereby singled out as being different from the other pupils. This difference amounted to a stigmatization by virtue of their religious followings.

The Court of Appeal agreed that peer pressure would cause the minority, non-Christian, children to conform to majority religious practices. The Court indicated that predominantly Christian practices are no longer acceptable to the community at large. The minority (non-Christians) should not be subjected to the religious observances espoused by the majority group. It was stated that the practices of reading scriptures, and reciting the Lord's Prayer in schools imposed Christian observances upon non-Christian students, thus violating the *Charter*. This was no longer permissible in Ontario.

Religious Readings and Prayer in British Columbia

In *Russow*, the plaintiffs also argued that their children had been discriminated against. They claimed that being "excused" from the daily reading of scriptures amounted to discrimination because their children were told to wait in the hallway without being assigned work (as the provincial regulation required). Furthermore, the children were the subjects of "taunts" by their peers as a result of such exclusion.

The British Columbia Supreme Court stated it would deal with this case as a freedom of religion issue and not one of discrimination. Although not bound by the Ontario ruling (*stare decisis*), the Court followed the *Zylberberg* ruling in reaching its decision, stating that it "would require a good deal of persuasion to reach an opposite conclusion to that of the majority" in the *Zylberberg* case. Portions of section 164 of the British Columbia *School Act* were hence ruled to contravene section 2(a) of the *Charter* and were extracted from the Act.

Section 164 of the Act now reads "all public schools shall be conducted on strictly secular and non-sectarian principles. The highest morality shall be inculcated but no religious dogma or creed shall be taught". The decision to remove Christian observances from schools has affected traditional practices within these school systems. Both Ontario and British Columbia have apparently adopted secular practices.

Religious Readings and Prayer in Manitoba

In August 1992 the Manitoba Court of Queen's Bench reached a similar conclusion as the courts in Ontario and British Columbia. The issue before the court was whether religious exercises should be permitted in a non-sectarian school system. In *Manitoba Association for Rights and Liberties et al. v. the Government of Manitoba et al.* (1992), a parent and a teacher (together with the Manitoba Association for Rights and Liberties Inc.) challenged sections 84(1), (2), (3), (4), (5), (6) and (7) of the *Public Schools Act*, which provided for practising religious exercises in public schools. They argued that such provisions violated sections 2 and 15 of the *Charter*.

The Court of Queen's Bench agreed with the plaintiffs, granting a declaration that the said provisions of the Act did indeed violate the *Charter*. The court relied heavily on the *Zylberberg* and *Russow* decisions, finding similar legislation infringed fundamental freedoms. Such violations could not be justified under section 1, hence non-compulsory religious exercises are unconstitutional in Manitoba public (non-denominational) schools.

Religious Curriculum and Indoctrination

It has been argued in *Corporation of the Canadian Civil Liberties Association v. Ontario (Elgin)* (1990) that religious freedom under the *Charter* prohibits Christian indoctrination. In this case, it was alleged that the school in Elgin County Ontario inculcated predominantly Christian values and that these values can no longer be the exclusive model for thought and behaviour within schools.

According to 1981 Census, Canada records over 90 per cent of some 70,000 inhabitants of Elgin County listed themselves as Christian. In 1986, the majority of parents of some 8,100 children enrolled in Elgin County's twenty-five elementary schools wanted some form of religious education for their children. Needless to say, parents who did not want their children to receive religious education had the option to have their children exempted from such teachings. Originally, religious teachings were exclusively Christian in nature but, by the time of this court hearing, this practice had changed.

In 1983, the Elgin County Board of Education took the initiative to revise its curriculum, including the teachings of other religious faiths besides Christianity in its curriculum. It was not until 1986, however, that the Board actually invited participation from various interested parties, in the form of submissions and briefs, to assist in further developing this new religious curriculum. In the school year 1986-87 the Board instituted a new religious curriculum that made references to religious faiths other than Christianity. But by this time the Corporation of the Canadian Civil Liberties Association had commenced legal proceedings against the Elgin County Board of Education, seeking an order:

- to declare s. 28 of Regulation 262, R.S.O. 1980, as amended, to be of no force or effect in consequence of its alleged infringement or denial of certain rights or freedoms guaranteed by the *Canadian Charter of Rights and Freedoms* ("the *Charter*");

- to declare the curriculum of religious studies prescribed by the respondent, The Elgin County Board of Education ("the Board") to be a denial of certain rights or freedoms guaranteed by the *Charter*; and,

- to enjoin the respondent, the Board, from continuing to require or permit its curriculum of religious studies to be offered in its schools. (71 O.R. (2d) p. 344)

Religious Indoctrination[1]

In 1990, the Ontario Court of Appeal held that section 28(4) of Regulation 262 under the Ontario *Education Act* was contrary to section 2(a) of the *Charter*. The Court also decided that the religious curriculum offered by

---

[1]   Holmes (1992), recognizing that defining indoctrination is very complex, discusses five different types of indoctrination: (1) The dictionary definition "to instruct in doctrines, principles, theories or beliefs, there being no apparent negative connotation" (p. 11). (2) The teaching of information where the learners are not "aware that they are being taught", or "aware of exactly what they are learning". This type, Holmes says, is sometimes referred to as brainwashing. (3) A third type "is that of teaching unprovable propositions" (p. 12). It is this definition that Holmes believes the court in the *Elgin* case was referring to in its verdict. (4) Indoctrination "as a form of instruction where the doctrine is simply taught and memorized" (p. 14). The doctrine must be "accepted without qualification". (5) "Teaching when there are core beliefs that cannot be successfully challenged" (p. 15).

the Elgin County Board of Education infringed religious freedoms under the *Charter*. The Court found that the curriculum focused largely on Christian doctrine, holding it out to be the exclusive means of modelling moral thinking and behaviours. Similar to the *Russow* and the *Zylberberg* cases, the Court concluded that "state authorized religious indoctrination amounts to the imposition of majoritian religious beliefs on minorities".

In reaching its decision, firstly, the Court examined historical background of the provincial legislation regarding religious instruction to determine its purpose. Upon examining various sources of data, including two comprehensive studies on religious education in Ontario public schools, it concluded the purpose of the provincial Regulation was to indoctrinate children, and the Elgin County curriculum reflected this intent. Secondly, the Court wanted to determine whether the exemption providing for children to be excused from religious instruction actually exempted these children from being indoctrinated, or exerted psychological pressure which inadvertently indoctrinated them.

The Court felt that students were still being indoctrinated in Christian dogma even though they were entitled to be exempted. In the words of Mr. Justice Austin, the Court agreed:

> that there is an appreciable degree of coercion or pressure on the personal applicants in this case. There is an inequality of situation by virtue of the nature of this programme. Accordingly, I am unable to agree with counsel for the board and for the Minister that the exempting provisions constitute a complete answer to any suggestion of coercion. (71 O.R. (2d) p. 363)

In short, the Court ruled that the purpose of this Regulation was to indoctrinate students with Christian morals and beliefs. The exemption provisions did nothing to deter this process of indoctrination. In fact, students who opted for exemption were "stigmatized as nonconformists". The Court stated that the minority religious group can no longer be subject to "the tyranny of the Christian majority". Religious indoctrination of this nature violates freedom of conscience and religion under section 2(a) of the *Charter of Rights and Freedoms*. Since the curriculum in the *Elgin* case does not constitute a "limit prescribed by law", the Court ruled that section 1 of the *Charter* does not apply. That is to say that such a violation is not permissible "in a free and democratic society".

Teaching About Religion

The Court in *Elgin* stated that schools cannot "indoctrinate" any one set of religious beliefs. It did rule, however, that schools may teach "about" religion. The Court of Appeal, in fact, outlined strategies to assist in distinguishing between religious indoctrination and education about religion.

The Eight-Point Test for Indoctrination

The judicially devised eight-point test specifically states:

1. The school may sponsor the *study* of religion, but may not sponsor the *practice* of religion.
2. The school may *expose* students to all religious views, but may not *impose* any particular view.
3. The school's approach to religion is one of *instruction*, not one of *indoctrination*.
4. The function of the school is to *educate* about religions, not to *convert* to any one religion.
5. The school's approach is *academic*, not *devotional*.
6. The school should study what all people believe, but should not *teach* a student what to believe.
7. The school should strive for student *awareness* of all religions, but should not press for student *acceptance* of any one religion.
8. The school should seek to *inform* the student about various beliefs, but should not seek to *conform* him or her to any one belief.

In order to comply with the ruling in the *Elgin* case the Government of Ontario instituted new regulations regarding religious education in public schools in Ontario.[2]

---

[2]   For further discussion on the *Elgin* case see: Black-Branch, J. L. (1992a) *Religious Instruction and the Tyranny of the Christian Majority*.   Paper presented to the Association for Moral Education, Toronto, Canada.

A Secular Curriculum in Ontario: Policy Memorandum 112

The new guidelines regarding religious education in public schools in Ontario came under Policy Memorandum 112 and Regulation 298. Essentially, sections 28 and 29 of Regulation 298 state that a board of education may provide "optional" programmes of education "about" religion. Such programmes are to "promote respect for the freedom of conscience and religion", as guaranteed under the *Charter*. They are to "provide for the study of different religions and religious beliefs" without giving primacy to any particular religion or belief. Moreover, religious indoctrination in any religion or belief is strictly prohibited.

The pith and substance of Regulation 298 was communicated to the chairpersons of boards of education, and school administrators in a policy memorandum. Policy Memorandum 112, entitled: "Education about Religion in the Public Elementary and Secondary Schools", spells out in no uncertain terms the Government's stand on its policy decision to secularize education in public schools in Ontario.

Challenging the Secular Curriculum in Ontario

The case of *Bal v. Ontario (Attorney General)* (1994) challenged the policy stand taken in Ontario. The plaintiffs, a group of parents from minority religious backgrounds, namely, Sikh, Hindu, Muslim, Mennonite and Dutch Reform, alleged that Policy Memorandum 112 and the corresponding Regulation 298 infringed their rights under section 2(a), section 2(b) and section 15 of the *Charter*. Consequently, they sought to have the memorandum and the Regulation struck down, to be of no force or effect, in accordance with section 52(1) of the *Constitution Act* 1982.

Analysing the issues, the Ontario Court (General Division) issued the following ruling. Firstly, Policy Memorandum 112 and Regulation 298 do not violate freedom of religion as per section 2(a). In order for it to infringe these rights, there must be "some state of coercion that denies or limits the exercise of one's religion". The Court ruled that regulations enforcing secularism were "neutral" in nature and thus there was no apparent coercion.

Secondly, the Court examined both the purpose and the effect of the policy memorandum and Regulation 298. In that regard, the purpose of the memorandum and the respective regulation was deemed to secularize the educational system, not to restrict expression. In addition, the effect was to "promote" secularism and not to restrict "expressive activities". As a result, the Court decided there was no infringement of the plaintiffs' freedom of expression under section 2(b), as alleged.

Thirdly, the Court dismissed the equality rights argument stating that it was not the secular educational system that imposed obligations, penalties or restrictive conditions on the applicants, but their choice of selecting that particular system for their children's education. That is to say, if the desire for religious education for their children was so great, the parents had the opportunity to send their children to religious schools, albeit with a cost.

In summary, the Ontario Court dismissed the *Charter* claims stating: "[t]hat to grant relief sought in this application would require that the Court undo what the Ontario Court of Appeal had decided in *Zylberberg*, *Elgin County* and *Adler*"[3] (21 O.R. (3d) p. 715). The General Division Court was not willing to undo these previous rulings.

Élitist Tendencies in Judicial Rulings: Religious Exercises and Curriculum

The rulings thus far on religious issues indicate the development of an élitist ideology in judicial interpretation of the *Charter*, one that carries through in relation to most *Charter*-related issues. That is, the judiciary seem to interpret the *Charter* in line with popular political sentiment at the time. The overall political mood in both Ontario and British Columbia at the time of the *Zylberberg*, *Elgin* and *Russow* rulings was one of secularism within non-denominational school settings.

Political parties in power at the time were espousing secularist views, except within established religious institutions such as the Roman Catholic separate school system which was a well entrenched, and indeed a politically accepted institution, at the time. In the rulings on religion in non-denominational schools, the courts made reference to what they called

---

3   The case of *Adler* is discussed in greater detail in Chapter Seven on denominational rights.

the "highest morality" within a secular system towards what all people believed. This implies that there actually exists a consensual, secular and universal code that is unconnected to religion. It supports the political ideology of the day, that "God is dead" in non-denominational schools and Canadians should march toward a "Godless state". Critics would contend that the indoctrination of a secularist view also comprises a dominant "world view" which inadvertently imposes a belief systems on the young, albeit from a different perspective.

Mandatory School Enrolment and Compulsory Attendance

The Canadian judiciary has stated that mandatory school enrolment and compulsory school attendance are necessary for "the education of the young". Judges are reluctant to rule against the existence of statutes and regulations which serve to govern school systems, such as those mandating school enrolment and attendance. They offer interpretations which perpetuate existing school structures. Further, courts support the infrastructure in place to regulate home schooling. Government bureaucracies are deemed secular in nature and of no religious affiliation.

School Enrolment and Attendance and Freedom Religion in Canada

In the case of *R. v. Jones* [1986], the accused refused to send his children to school as required by section 142(1) of the Alberta *School Act*. Jones believed that it was his God-given right to educate his children at home. Similarly, he did not believe that he should adhere to the bureaucratic procedures required in order to obtain permission for home instruction or opening a private school.

   At that time Jones was operating his own school, "Western Baptist Academy", which was not registered with the Department of Education in Alberta. He was teaching his own three children and approximately twenty others in the basement of his church. Pastor Jones believed, and argued, that he alone had authority from God to see to his children's education. He thought it would be sinful to request state permission for home instruction as outlined in the Alberta *School Act*, under section 143(1)(a), a provision allowing for certification for home instruction. In addition to violating his religious freedoms, he claimed that compulsory certification indicating that a pupil is "under efficient instruction" (as required by the province) violated his entitlement to liberty and fundamental justice, under section 7 of the *Charter*. Moreover, he argued that having to apply to open a private school under section 143(1)(e) of the Act further contravened his freedom of religion under section 2(a).

The Supreme Court of Canada ruled that the pertinent sections of the *School Act* contravened neither Jones' section 2(a) freedom of conscience and religion, nor the principles of fundamental justice. The Court stated that the *School Act* "does not have a religious purpose". The purpose of laws governing education is to ensure "the education of the young". The Court stated that the existing provisions merely regulate education and are secular in nature. The Court acknowledged that there are provisions in the Act allowing for alternative arrangements (i.e., home instruction or opening a private school) for those people who do not favour the existing provincial provisions for education. It ruled that it was Jones' personal decision not to follow the minimum requirements of the Act in order to take these alternative measures. The Court concluded that the protection of rights can only be "within the limits of reason". "To permit anyone to ignore it [the Act] on the basis of religious conviction would create an unwarranted burden on the operation of a legitimate legislative scheme to assure a reasonable standard of education."

School Attendance and Equality Rights

Following the Supreme Court decision, Jones was charged once again for failing to comply with the compulsory attendance provisions under section 142 of the Albert *School Act*. In the case of *R. v. Jones* (1987), he argued that the *School Act* violated his freedom of religion under the Alberta *Bill of Rights*. In addition, he argued that the *School Act* contravened the equality rights provisions under the *Charter*, for all provinces have different systems of education and therefore they are not all equal.

The Alberta Provincial Court found Jones guilty as charged for failing to see that his child attend school. The Court stated that the *School Act* does not violate the Alberta *Bill of Rights*. The "legislation governing education has no religious orientation". Secondly, there was no *Charter* violation. For although education as prescribed under the Alberta *School Act* may differ from that of other provinces, both in structure and administration, that in itself did not constitute a breach of equality rights. All provinces are attempting to reach the same end, that is, the education of the young. Differences in achieving this end do not in themselves constitute discrimination.

Opening a Private School and Freedom Religion in Alberta

Similar to the Supreme Court ruling in the initial case of *Jones* was the case of *Bienert* (1985). Both took place in Alberta and involved issues regarding compulsory school attendance, certification for home instruction and authorization to operate a private school. In *R. v. Bienert* (1985), Pastor Bienert of the Fox Creek Chapel, was also charged with operating a school without ministerial approval, in accordance with section 10(3) of the *School Act*. In this case, Bienert also argued religious grounds for operating this private school without prior authorization from the Department of Education in Alberta. He also claimed that the legislation requiring him to register the school violated his religious freedoms.

   The Court agreed there had been a *prima facie* violation of the pastor's section 2(a) freedoms. But, referring to section 1 of the *Charter*, the limitations clause, the judiciary stated it was justifiable to limit Bienert's freedoms and make him comply with the *School Act* in order to gain private school status. The pertinent sections of the Alberta *School Act*, did indeed provide justifiable limits "prescribed by law" to Pastor Bienert's religious freedoms, which were reasonable "in a free and democratic society".

School Attendance in Saskatchewan

In the case of in *R. v. Kotelmach and Kotelmach* (1989) the parents of a school-age child were charged and convicted on two counts of failing to ensure that their child attended school on a regular basis. Andrew and Diane May Kotelmach alleged that attendance policies under section 155 of the *Education Act* effectively violated their *Charter* rights. They argued, *inter alia*, that in light of their constitutional rights as per sections

2, 7, 15 and 27 of the *Charter*, as well as provincial human rights legislation, the trial judge had erred in law when he convicted them.

The Saskatchewan Court of Queen's Bench limited the issues to section 2 and section 7 of the *Charter*. In that regard the Court stated that the compulsory attendance policy pursuant to section 155 of the Act did not infringe the rights of the parents to educate their child as they saw fit, as per section 7, the right to life, liberty and security of the person. The very fact that they were faced with a penalty for failing to ensure their child's attendance at school did not in itself constitute a deprivation of rights within the meaning of section 7.

The Court did, however, state that the compulsory attendance policy may "somewhat infringe" one's freedom of religion, as per section 2. But such an infringement was demonstrably justifiable under section 1 of the *Charter*. Whilst the existing legislation may not have provided the education desired by the Kotelmachs, equally it did not preclude them from making alternative arrangements such as enrolling their child in a religious school, or indeed, providing home instruction. The case was thus dismissed and the conviction upheld. At that time, in the Province of Saskatchewan, a fine of $100 was levied for the first offence of neglecting to ensure regular attendance of one's child, $250 for the second, and $500 for the third and subsequent offences.

School Enrolment in Newfoundland

In *R. v. Arbeau* (1986), the father of a school-age child claimed that the provision under the *School Act* which stipulates that every person who takes up residence in Newfoundland and has a child "shall present that child for [school] enrolment", contravened his *Charter* rights under sections 2(a), 7, and 11(d).

The Newfoundland Court of Appeal decided that mandatory school enrolment, under the Act, does not contravene section 2(a), freedom of religion. Nor does it contravene section 7, (life, liberty, and security of person), or section 11(d), (the right to be presumed innocent until proven guilty), under the *Charter*. The Court stated that even if section 6(2) of the Act, regarding mandatory school enrolment, did contravene these *Charter* provisions, such limits could be "demonstrably justified in a free and democratic society" under section 1 of the *Charter*.

The case of *R. v. McCloud and Randell* (1987) also dealt with the issue of mandatory school enrolment in Newfoundland. In this case the Supreme Court of Newfoundland followed the *Arbeau* decision, ruling in favour of compulsory school attendance.   The parents, charged with failing to enrol their children in school under section 6(2) of the *School Act*, pleaded this section of the Act was unconstitutional and contrary to section 15 of the *Charter*. Earlier, a lower court had agreed with the parents' claim, acquitting them of the charges. The Supreme Court of Newfoundland, however, reversed the acquittal. The Court upheld the constitutionality of section 6(2), stating the previous judge had erred in accepting the section 15 argument.

School Attendance and "Needing" a Child at Home

In the case of *R. v. Jomaa* (1987), an Alberta Provincial Court rejected a section 7 *Charter* argument saying that section 180(1) of the Alberta *School Act*, (imposing a penalty for a parent whose child is truant) does not contravene principles of fundamental justice under the *Charter*. The parents argued that the daughter was needed at home to tend to such domestic chores as looking after her siblings; cooking; tending to guests of the family; and, tending to other family "matters" and "affairs".[4]

School Attendance and the Presumption of Innocence

In *R. v. Prentice* (1985) an Ontario Provincial Court found the parents guilty of refusing to send their child to school, rejecting a section 11(d) *Charter* argument. They argued a violation of their "right to be presumed innocent until proven guilty according to law in a fair and public hearing by an independent and impartial tribunal". The parents failed to provide evidence of adequate home instruction.

---

[4]   In the case of *Jomaa* it was also ruled that the charge of failing to require a child to attend school is a strict liability offence. The defence of reasonable care applies thereto.

Home Instruction and Bible Teachings

In the case of *R. v. Powell* (1985) a section 2(a) *Charter* argument was rejected by an Alberta Provincial Court regarding compulsory school attendance. The parents were charged with two counts of truancy in accordance with section 180(1) of the *School Act*. The parents admitted that the chronic absences of their children was because they were not interested in keeping their children in the school system. Initially, they had rejected any form of alternative schooling or home instruction.

They eventually submitted a proposal for home instruction which related strictly to "the teachings of the Bible". The Court rejected the plan stating that it could not "allow a proliferation and acceleration of unapproved sub-standard home study espoused by splintered religious factions". The Court emphasized that section 143 of the *School Act*, mandating compulsory school attendance, did not offend the parents' freedom of conscience or religion, or the rules of fundamental justice.

Home Schooling and Arbitrary Decision-Making in Newfoundland

In a slightly different case from the above mentioned *Bienert* and *Jones*, in *R. v. Kind* (1984), a parent was willing to follow the state-set procedures to offer home instruction to his daughter. Kind was, in fact, certified as a grade two teacher. He had applied for permission to teach his daughter at home and the superintendent denied the request. The superintendent stated that the programme to be offered by Kind would not be equivalent to all aspects of the existing school program.

Kind subsequently withdrew his child from school and commenced home instruction, against the will of the school superintendent. He was subsequently charged and convicted by a Provincial Court for not having his child attend school in accordance with the Newfoundland *School Attendance Act*. Kind argued a violation of his fundamental justice under section 7.

The Newfoundland District Court acquitted Kind of the charges, maintaining that indeed he had been "denied" his right to life, liberty and security of person. The Court acknowledged that a statutory provision, section 8(d) of the *School Attendance Act*, allows for home instruction. The Court stated that to allow a one-man tribunal (on the part of the superintendent) to make a decision of this nature, based on his assessment that the programme offered would not be equivalent in all aspects of the school program, renders section 8(d) "meaningless" and denies the applicant fundamental justice. In addition, the Court stated that the child was under competent instruction at home and Kind had complied with the Act.

Home Schooling and Arbitrary Decision-Making in Saskatchewan

In the case of Elizabeth Cline (in the unreported) case of *R. v. Cline* (1988) her *Charter* argument regarding home schooling was upheld. Cline had made all the necessary arrangements to home school her son Eric but the director of education (as required by the province at that time) refused to consider the programme submitted.

Charged with failing to send her son to school, she argued (with the support of an expert witness) that her son was receiving an adequate education at home. Moreover, Cline said that her failure to comply with section 155 of the Saskatchewan *Education Act* was legitimate because of the director's breach of duties in regard to her application to home school her son. She argued this failure to do so violated her principles of fundamental justice under section 7 of the *Charter*.

The Provincial Court of Saskatchewan agreed with Cline stating: "the exercise of the director of education's discretion in the approval or non-approval of a home programme must be exercised fairly and cannot be exercised arbitrarily". The Court thus found a breach of section 7, dismissing the truancy charges laid against Cline.

Home Instruction and Discretionary Powers

Similar to the *Kind* case, it appeared in *Cline* that an individual holding discretionary powers (i.e., the school superintendent and the director of education, respectively) wanted the said children to attend the regular school system, hence making an arbitrary decision which violated parental rights. In the other cases pertaining to school enrolment and attendance, it would appear that the parents were reluctant to take the necessary steps to attain permission to home instruct. The courts are emphatically sending the message that they will support the infrastructure in place to uphold the educational system, even if they must invoke section 1 to do so, but, as illustrated in *Cline* and *Kind*, they will not support arbitrary decision-making. Whilst taking these decisions, administrators must be prepared to be fair and impartial. They must not be shaded by their personal preferences as to how children should be educated.

Élitist Tendencies in Judicial Rulings: Control Over Schooling

In sum, the above cases focused predominantly on the constitutionality of specific regulations requiring compulsory school enrolment and attendance. Such judicial decisions have a number of direct implications for schools at the provincial level in that they uphold the legislative schemes (the infrastructure of school systems) currently in place. The decisions, particularly that of *Jones*, both support and perpetuate the idea of state authority over education.

Mandatory school enrolment is a means by which the state has control over all children. It ensures they are registered in educational institutions, which are strictly regulated. Compulsory school attendance expands the scope of state control in that schools can insist that children attend regularly. That is to say, not only must all children enrol in school (unless the parents have made other arrangements) but, children must attend school regularly (unless there are legitimate reasons as to why they cannot). Those wanting their children to engage in alternative forms of schooling must conform to state-set guidelines, where the courts have upheld a large degree of state control. This reiterates the notion of the courts interpreting and enforcing the *Charter* in a manner which supports the political *status quo*, that education is "necessary" and for the "good" of society.

They are only willing to rule against the system where there has been an obvious abuse of power by an administrator who has exceeded his or her powers, thus acting in an arbitrary manner, such as in the cases of *Kind* and *Cline*. But more often than not even when there is a *prima facie* violation of an individuals rights, such as in the cases of *Jones*, *Bienert* and other, the judiciary are more than willing to bend to popular political sentiment and maintain educational statutes enacted by politicians, even if it means invoking the limitations clause under section 1 in order to do so.

Mandatory Membership in a Teachers' Federation

The courts did not lend a sympathetic ear to the request of teachers concerning mandatory membership in a teachers' federation. In fact, the Court in the case of *Spier v. Burnaby Board of School Trustees, District No. 41* (1988) maintained the *status quo*. In that case, a group of teachers applied for an injunction restraining their termination of employment for refusing to join the British Columbia Teachers' Association and the British Columbia Teachers' Federation.

The request came as a result of Bill 20, the new collective bargaining régime requiring mandatory membership in the British Columbia Teachers' Federation. Teachers refusing to join would face termination of their employment. The plaintiffs claimed that mandatory membership infringed their freedom of conscience and religion, and freedom of association under section 2(a) and section 2(d) respectively of the *Charter*. The Court did not allow the injunction, stating "these teachers have had to live with the situation for a very long time; for them that has always been the *status quo* either by virtue of the *School Act*, or now, by virtue of the collective agreement". As a result, the Court said the applicants could wait until the case went to trial.

Cases involving whether a court should grant an interim injunction tend to involve issues regarding "irreparable harm" and "the balance of convenience". In such cases, regardless of the overall issue, courts tend to favour the *status quo*. They prefer to leave the substantive questions to the trial court (as in this case) and not "grant the remedy in advance".

Freedom of Expression and the Teachers' Code of Ethics

The British Columbia Court of Appeal has ruled that teachers can be reprimanded for breaching a code of ethics involving personal criticism directed at another teacher. In the case of *Cromer v. British Columbia Teachers' Federation* [1986], one teacher criticized another teacher at a public meeting. Madeleine Sauve, a guidance teacher, had "developed a guidance programme dealing with human sexuality". Complaints were lodged against the programme and subsequently a public meeting was held to discuss the programme.

At the meeting, Cromer who was both a parent as well as a grade six teacher in the same school district, criticized Sauve saying something to the effect that, "Sauve should not be a teacher or a guidance counsellor if she treats children like she does their parents" and "Sauve needs to learn appropriate skills for dealing with parents".

Rule 5 of the British Columbia Teachers' Code of Ethics provides that "any criticism of the teaching performance and related duties of a colleague must be directed to the colleague personally and, only then, after informing the colleague of the intent to do so, should criticism be directed to appropriate officials". Sauve charged Cromer with a breach of this Code of Ethics.

The British Columbia Court of Appeal stated that freedom of expression under the *Charter* can potentially override the Code of Ethics. In this particular instance, however, personal criticism directed at another teacher, and not the subject matter of a meeting, was sufficient reason for disciplinary action in accordance with a breach of the Code of Ethics. Mr. Justice Lambert stated that freedom of expression was not absolute, requiring a "balancing of interests" between the Code of Ethics and Cromer's interests.

Lambert J. saw the balance in this case to weigh towards the Code of Ethics because Cromer had directed "personal" criticism directly at Sauve and not the subject matter the teacher was discussing *per se*. Lambert J. stated that such instances of personal criticism directed at colleagues "come squarely within the public interest that brought clauses of the Code of Ethics into being" in the first place. Individual freedom of expression is not absolute and interests will be balanced according to individual situations.

Freedom of Expression and Parental Access to Schools

Serup v. Board of Trustees of School District # 57 et al. (1987) dealt with the rights of parents and administrative policies and decision-making autonomy. Serup, the mother of a teenage son attending a high school in Prince George, British Columbia, habitually visited the school library, canvassing the books and at times signing them out for further review. In 1983, she complained to the school board that one book in particular was inappropriate for the school library because it dealt with topics on "boys and sex".

Again in 1984 she made similar complaints regarding a book on "girls and sex". At this point the school principal informed her that she could only visit the library and remove books with his permission. Serup sought a mandatory injunction allowing her to continue her past practices. She argued that being refused entry to her child's school library violated her freedom of expression under the *Charter*. She claimed she held the right to enter the school library at will to look at, remove, and review books.

The Court stated that Serup had neither been prevented from "entering the school" nor had she been prevented from "expressing herself". The Court pointed out that she was permitted to enter the school to survey and remove books but now she needed special administrative permission in order to do so. To enter without administrative permission would be an inappropriate intrusion on the administration of the school. The Court stated: "The Board has a statutory obligation to educate and it must do so in ways it sees fit." The judge ruled that the principal's actions did not violate Serup's section 2 freedom of expression and if such a violation did occur, it was saved by the limitations clause of section 1 of the *Charter*.

Élitist Tendencies in Judicial Rulings: Control Over Content

The ruling in *Serup* is another in the series which upholds the political ideology of the day. It is well accepted that schools must do what they are intended to do, without undue, or perhaps one should say "unpopular" parental outcry. That is to say, issues of sex education, or at least, having a school library stocked with appropriate information in matters pertaining thereto, is well accepted within Canadian society at large. Indeed it is safe to say that it is, to some degree, expected. In this case the Court was willing to invoke the limitations clause if it was necessary to uphold the popular sentiment that administrators must do what they have to in order to ensure the "proper" education of children. "Proper" is defined as that which is politically acceptable and education about sex is politically acceptable at this point.

Freedom of Expression and School Dress Codes

In *Devereux v. Lambton County (Roman Catholic Separate School Board)* (1988) the Court rejected a student's claim that a school imposed dress code violated his freedom of expression (under section 2(b)) of the *Charter*, liberty (section 7) and equality (section 15). The student argued that the "casual uniform" requirement adopted by the Lambton County Roman Catholic Separate School Board infringed his said constitutional rights.

The Court ruled that the Board had the power to institute a policy regarding "Student Attire". Further, any such violation would be saved by section 1 of the *Charter* -- being within reasonable limits on individual freedoms and rights. It stated: "to hold otherwise would be to trivialize those rights" under the *Charter*. The Court did not rely on the denominational status of the School Board when reaching its decision, hence having implications for all publicly funded schools (both denominational and non-denominational).

Freedom of Religion and School Dress Codes in Public Schools

In contrast to the decision in *Devereux v. Lambton County* regarding dress codes the courts have ruled against school policies restricting the wearing of ceremonial daggers (Kirpans) for Khalsa Sikhs in publicly funded schools. In *Ontario (Human Rights Commissioner) v. Peel (Board of Education)* (1991) it was decided that a "no-weapons" policy enacted by Peel Board, which effectively prohibited the wearing of Kirpans (as they were classified as weapons which could be dangerous in certain circumstance) was in violation of the Human Rights Code of Ontario. The Commission ordered the policy to be withdrawn, subject to some safety restrictions.[5]

Freedom of Religion and School Dress Codes in Private Schools

In a case involving a private school, a Human Rights Commission Board

---

[5]   In *Ontario v. Peel,* leave to the Ontario Court of Appeal was refused.

of Inquiry heard the case of *Sehdev v. Bayview Glen Junior Schools Ltd.* (1988) in which a Sikh student claimed the school dress code violated his *Charter* rights. The Court ruled that the private school's mandatory dress code discriminated against Sikh religious dress requirements. The school was ordered to change its policy.

Élitist Tendencies in Judicial Rulings: Dress Codes

It is important to note that the cases of *Sehdev* and *Peel* involved the issue of religious dress (be they in private or public educational settings). The decisions in these cases reflect the dominant ideology that freedom of religion entails freedom of religious dress. This coincides with the current political position of Canadian multiculturalism. In the case of *Devereux*, however, he was denied the right to assert his freedom of expression based on personal freedom. Hence from these cases it would appear that the courts support the administrative policies of schools when it involves personal preference but they will not support those policies (be they in private or public settings) which restrict religious freedoms. From these rulings, it seems that students must be attired in appropriate school uniforms, unless they restrict or deny religious freedoms within a multicultural, multi-denominational Canada.[6]

Students' Freedom of Expression and Speech

The case of *Lutes v. Board of Education of Prairie View School Division No. 74* (1992) involved questions of freedom of speech for students and school-sanctioned discipline. Chris Lutes, a grade nine student, received a month of noon hour detentions for singing the song "Let's Talk About Sex". At the time, Lutes was on his lunch hour recess and was off school grounds (on Prairie Avenue in Milestone, Saskatchewan).

---

[6]   It may be said that upholding religious dress codes, particularly for Muslim women, is, in fact, a violation of the rights of the minority in that such dress codes inadvertently ghettoize and oppress them within a broader societal context. Their religious dress effectively serves to marginalize them from society by singling them out as different, hence stigmatizing them. The wearing of such clothing is restricted in state-run schools in France.

He sang the song in front of a school division official (Richard Buettner) knowing full well that the song had been banned at the school level. Offended by the action, Buettner reported the singing to the Vice-Principal of Lutes' school who promptly disciplined Lutes by issuing a month of noon hour detentions.

Lutes applied to the court for an interim injunction to prohibit the school from enforcing the punishment. He argued that the rap song, by the American group "Salt 'N' Pepa", was not offensive. It actually promotes safe sex practices in an age of growing concerns regarding the spread of the AIDS virus. In fact, many schools in the United States currently promote the song in order to convey this exact message.

The school held its ground arguing that regardless of the nature of the song, it was banned by the school and Lutes was thus defying school orders. In essence, he was being punished for breaching the discipline code. In addition, the school stated that Lutes was subject to disciplinary action even though he was on his lunch hour and off school property. The fact that Lutes was bussed to school rendered him under the supervision of the school from the moment he entered the school bus until he stepped off in the late afternoon. Hence, in accordance with section 150(b) of the Saskatchewan *Education Act*, Lutes was subject to supervision and in effect, disciplinary actions. Once again, the school argued that Lutes was not disciplined for expressing himself but was disciplined for his rude and disrespectful behaviour to a school official.

The Saskatchewan Court of Queen's Bench agreed that curtailing Lutes from singing the song was a *prima facie* violation of his *Charter* freedoms under section 2(b). Further, this violation could not be saved by section 1. But the judge stated that these issues would have to be settled at trial. This particular hearing was to determine whether an injunction should be granted to rest the disciplinary action until after the issues were decided at trial.

Since there was no firm evidence to suggest that Lutes would suffer irreparable harm if compelled to finish the month of detentions (at which time there were five days left to complete), the court dismissed the request for the injunction. Lutes was, however, entitled to proceed with his action against the school and to seek damages for the school having infringed his freedom of expression.

Freedom of Speech and the Promotion of Hatred

The *Keegstra* case was an example of limiting a former teacher's freedom of speech. James Keegstra was a high school teacher in Alberta who was dismissed from his teaching duties in 1982. His dismissal was directly related to his inculcation of hatred against Jewish people whilst teaching history. In *Keegstra v. Lacombe County 14 (Board of Education)* [1983] a Board of Reference moved to dismiss Keegstra from his teaching position for ignoring the lawful instructions of the School Board. The Board of Reference felt that his dismissal was "sufficiently justified" in that he "failed to comply" with the "specific directives" from the School Board. Keegstra was subsequently charged with promoting hatred against Jews.[7]

The 1988 Alberta Court of Appeal, in *R. v. Keegstra*, stated that section 281.2 of the *Criminal Code* (prohibiting the promotion of hatred against an identifiable group) violated Keegstra's freedom of speech, as guaranteed under section 2(b) of the *Charter*. The Court said that section 2(b) protects both innocent error and imprudent speech and therefore, section 1 of the *Charter* did not override the respondent's rights.

The Supreme Court of Canada ruling, however, reversed this decision in *R. v. Keegstra* (1990). The Court examined whether section 281.2 of the *Criminal Code* (prohibiting the promotion of hatred against an identifiable group) violated the defendant's freedom of speech as guaranteed under section 2(b) and section 11(d) (the presumption of innocence) of the *Charter*. The Court stated: "although the reverse onus provision contained in s. 319 (3)(a) . . . (of the *Criminal Code*) . . . conflicts with the s. 11(d) . . . (of the *Charter of Rights*) . . . presumption of innocence, it can be seen as a justifiable means of excusing truthful statements without undermining the objective of preventing harm caused by the intentional promotion of hatred". That being the case, although section 319(3)(a) of the *Criminal Code* violates the *Charter*, this contravention of section 11(d) is justifiable under section 1 of the *Charter*.[8]

---

7   Some of Keegstra's former students testified that he taught them that "Jews were evil, determined to destroy Christianity and bent on controlling the world" ("Keegstra conviction struck down" [Toronto] *Globe and Mail*, 1994, 8 September).

8   After being twice found guilty of wilfully promoting hatred against Jews, the Keegstra affair continues as he tries to have his conviction overturned on the basis that he

The Keegstra affair has had a profound effect on education in Alberta. Changes include an amendment to the Alberta Teachers' Association Code of Ethics and the establishment of a Council on Alberta Teacher Standards.[9]

Freedom of Speech and Private Beliefs

The case of *Ross v. Moncton Board of School Trustees, District No. 15* (1993) involved issues of freedom of expression outside the classroom. Ross, a teacher in Moncton, New Brunswick, made anti-Jewish statements and participated in actions to that effect in his private life. A New Brunswick Board of Inquiry found that there was no evidence to suggest "any direct classroom activity by Malcolm Ross" on which the complaint was based. Nevertheless, the Board found that these extra-school activities did indeed violate the New Brunswick *Human Rights Act*. Although Ross was not working in a classroom teaching situation at the time of the hearing, the Board of Inquiry found the School Board guilty of unintentional discrimination by continuing to employ Ross.

An order was then issued against the New Brunswick Department of Education and the Moncton School Board. In particular, the Board of Inquiry directed the School Board to:

(a) place Ross on a leave of absence without pay for the period of 18 months; (b) appoint him to a non-teaching position, if one became available during that period; (c) terminate his employment at the end of that period if, in the interim, he had not been offered and accepted a non-teaching position; and, (d) terminate his employment with the School Board immediately if he published or wrote anti-Semitic materials or sold his previous publications any time during the leave of absence period or at any time during his employment in a non-teaching position.

did not receive a fair trial. In fact, on 7 September 1994, in *R. v. Keegstra*, the Alberta Court of Appeal decided by a vote of 2-1 that he had not been given a fair trial and his conviction cannot stand. See the article "Keegstra conviction struck down" [Toronto] *Globe and Mail*, (1994, September, 8).

[9] For further reading on the Keegstra affair see: "A Trust Betrayed: The Keegstra Affair", Bercuson and Wertheimer (1987).

The New Brunswick Court of Appeal overturned the Board of Inquiry ruling stating that sections (a), (b) and (c) of the order violated Ross's right to freedom of religion and expression as per sections 2(a) and (b) of the *Charter* and such violations could not be justified under section 1, the limitations clause. Ross was to be re-instated as a teacher, with the Court stating that, "the purpose behind the order [removing him from the class-room] is not so pressing and substantial as to justify overriding constitutionally guaranteed rights. It was the appellant's activities outside the class-room that were the basis of the complaint. . . . To uphold the order would have the effect of condoning the suppression of views that are not politically popular at any given time" (p. 242, 110 D.L.R. (4th)).

The Supreme Court of Canada, however, overturned the New Brunswick Court of Appeal ruling. Specifically, clauses (a), (b) and (c) of the Board of Inquiry's Order were properly made within the Board's jurisdiction. Further, any resulting infringement of Ross's rights to freedom of religion or expression would be justifiably limited under section 1 of the *Charter*.

In reference to the affair, the Court stated:

> The continued employment of the respondent [Ross] contributed to an invidiously discriminatory or "poisoned" educational environment, as established by the evidence and the Board's finding that it was "reasonable to anticipate" that the respondent's writings and statements influenced the anti-Semitic sentiment. In my opinion, this finding is necessarily linked to the finding that the respondent's statements are "highly public" and that he is a notorious anti-Semite, as well as the supported view that public school teachers assume a position of influence and trust over their students and must be seen to be impartial and tolerant.

The judgement of the Court of Appeal was thus reversed.[10]

---

10   An example concerning the issue of role modelling and freedom of expression for teachers is the recent case in Peel Board of Education, Ontario where Paul Fromme, a teacher with the Board, is a member of a neo-fascist group. Unlike James Keegstra or Malcolm Ross, he has kept a relatively low profile in his activities. There appears to be no evidence that his teaching ability has been affected. There is no evidence that the environment in the school has been affected. He has taught a large number of multicultural students and there has never been a complaint.

Fundamental Freedoms Conclusions

A number of important pointers emanate from the above discussed cases. Firstly, it appears that non-denominational schools are moving more into a secular domain. As a result, it would seem that courts will generally be supportive of efforts which do not impose Christian prayers and readings on children in non-denominational schools. They are likely to embrace efforts which are inclusive of all religious denominations, faiths and belief systems. In the event of a non-denominational school system deciding to include religious issues in school activities, courts are more likely to support ones which do not impose activities on students which are predominantly Christian in nature. The judiciary has promoted, and hence is likely to support, the use of the eight-point test whilst interpreting religious teachings.

Secondly, school enrolment is mandatory. It would seem that all children must be registered with a local school or within a board of education. In addition, they must attend regularly. School attendance is compulsory (unless arrangements have been made to home school).

Thirdly, in order to gain judicial support, parents or guardians wishing to home school their children must adhere to guidelines set by provincial ministries of education. These vary from province to province. Local school board officials will be able to offer up-to-date advice regarding procedures and regulations. Administrative decisions regarding permission to home school must be made on a fair and impartial basis.

Fourthly, courts seem likely to examine issues of freedom of speech and expression for students. Students should be permitted to express themselves freely. Whilst they are indeed required to adhere to school rules and disciplinary expectations, educators must be reasonable both when setting rules and when administering sanctions for violations thereof. It is quite clear from the courts that students must follow disciplinary codes as set by the schools, including dress codes, unless they violate religious rights.

Fifthly, teachers must also adhere to certain principles, such as those enshrined in codes of ethics and the *Charter*. In order to maintain professional standards, teachers must be reasonable when speaking against colleagues. Whilst teachers are guaranteed a wide latitude of personal freedoms pertaining to their private lives, they cannot exhibit personal beliefs in the classroom with the intent of indoctrinating students about alternative views and lifestyles which are not espoused by the school system, particularly ones of a religious nature (it should be noted that gay and lesbian issues are likely to be viewed substantially different from those relating to anti-semitism or white supremacy).[11]

In sum, it seems that fundamental freedoms, as they pertain to schools, means being free to be an individual, be it in belief, expression or association, without imposing such ideologies on others.

---

[11]   An Ontario Human Rights Tribunal in the *Leshner* case has already recognized same sex conjugal relationships as equal to those of heterosexuals. In fact, since August of 1992, homosexuals have made four giant leaps in extending their rights. In August, the Federal Court of Canada ruled that the *Human Rights Act of Canada* protects homosexuals. In September, the above mentioned Human Rights tribunal in *Leshner*, ordered the Province of Ontario to drop the phrase "opposite sex" from its definition of marital status. In October of 1992, the Canadian Armed Forces agreed to stop discriminating against gays. In December of 1992 (then) Federal Minister of Justice, Kim Campbell, announced that she would include the protection of homosexuals under the wording of the *Canadian Human Rights Act*.

4 Legal Rights

Introduction

The granting of constitutional rights to students, parents and teachers is a very new phenomenon within the educational sector. School administrators formerly enjoyed a large degree of administrative autonomy in their decision-making capacity. Parental and student intervention were not unusual, but court challenges to an educator's authority were rare. It is safe to say that school administrators made decisions according to what they felt was appropriate for the safety, security and well-being of the school environment. They made decisions that were deemed to be in the "best interest of the child" and to the school community at large. Although there was, and still is, significant legislative control, administrators were virtually exempt from judicial intervention, particularly regarding issues of discipline.

Traditional Judicial Deference

Other than in extreme circumstances, courts were reluctant to deal with issues of student discipline. Dickinson and MacKay (1989) report that

> the traditional approach of Canadian courts to the matter of students' procedural rights in school discipline cases has been to defer almost completely to school officials' discretion and to prefer the virtues of discipline and obedience over those associated with individual rights and challenging authority. (p. 318)

The cases of *McIntyre v. The Public School Trustees of Section Eight in the Township of Blanchard et al.* (1886) and *Re Ward and Board of Blaine Lake School* (1971) perfectly illustrate judicial deference to the discretion of school administrators. In *McIntyre* the Court upheld the dismissal of a student from school until he apologized for his "disobedience". The student argued this requirement denied him his right to attend school. Mr. Justice Cameron stated that the condition stipulating the student apologize was "a reasonable one" and he was not being denied his legal rights. It was, in effect, his fear of being humiliated -- and thus his not apologizing -- that denied him his attending school, not the provision to apologize itself.

Eighty-five years later, the judiciary in the case of *Ward* reiterated the reluctance of the courts to become involved in affairs regarding student discipline. In this case, a student was suspended from school for wearing his hair too long. Issues in question were the validity of the School Board regulation stipulating hair styles for males, and the question of natural justice for the student in question.

The Court held that the School Board regulation regarding hair styles was valid, and the Board decision to temporarily suspend the student until he obeyed the regulation was also valid. Natural justice, at that time, applied only in judicial decisions and the School Board was acting in an administrative capacity. In essence, it was within the powers of the Board to administer and manage the educational affairs of the school district and to exercise a general supervision and control over the schools of the Board. The student had no "clear legal right" to attend school until he complied with the Board's mandate.

Discipline and the Exertion of Physical Force Over Students

Based on an assessment of many court cases dealing with incidents involving students and administrative practices judges are likely to uphold administrative and teacher actions that are thought to be in the overall interest of the school community. Some of these instances involve the physical handling of students.

In the case of *R. v. Lauzon* (1991), heard by a Provincial Court in Ontario, a high school teacher was charged with two counts of assault, stemming from incidents in the gymnasium and the boys' locker room. In this incident the teacher admitted to using physical force -- grabbing the student's arm several times and shaking him -- for belligerent language and defiance of authority. The judge upheld the teacher's actions, referring to section 43 of the *Criminal Code* and stating that the teacher did not use "excessive force" whilst "trying to control and remove a defiant, recalcitrant, rebellious student". Commenting on this case, Dickinson (1992) states:

> The *Lauzon* case illustrates perfectly . . . that protection of the rights of others in the learning environment requires authorizing teachers to forcibly discipline those who disrupt that environment. Even the Law Reform Commission of Canada, which has recommended the repeal of section 43 of the *Criminal Code*, would not interfere with teachers' authority to use coercive or restraining force. (p. 230)

In fact, Dickinson says that "perceptions about the law's intolerance for the use of physical force in school discipline are simply wrong". He states there are "dozens" of cases that prove this point, citing the cases of: *R. v. Gaul* (1904); *R. v. Metcalfe* (1927); *Murdock v. Richards* [1954]; *R. v. Haberstock* (1970); and, *R. v. Dimmell* (1980) to illustrate his point. Please note that many of these cases are pre-*Charter* cases and did not deal with *Charter*-related arguments.

Traditional Authority to Legal-Bureaucratic Authority

Many administrators feel that in recent years much of their traditional authority and decision-making autonomy has been replaced by legal-bureaucratic authority.[1]

Traditional Authority

"*Traditional authority* is anchored in an established belief in the sanctity of the status of those exercising authority in the past. Obedience is owed to the traditionally sanctioned *position* of authority, and the person who occupies the position inherits the authority established by custom. In a school, for example, students may accept the authority of the position and

[1]   These forms of authority are based on the notions as first proposed by Max Weber.

the teacher because their parents and grandparents did so before them"
(Hoy & Miskel, 1987, p. 110).

Legal-Bureaucratic Authority

"*Legal authority* is based on enacted laws that can be changed by formally
correct procedures. Obedience is not owed to a person or position *per se*
but to the *laws* that specify to whom and to what extent people owe
compliance. Legal authority thus extends only within the scope of the
authority vested in the office by law. In a school obedience is owed to the
impersonal principles that govern the operation of the organization" (Hoy
& Miskel, 1987, p. 110).

The Erosion of the Doctrine of *in loco parentis*

There is little doubt amongst most educators that schools have become
more bureaucratized with legal authority taking a firm hold. In recent
years there have been more ministerial regulations, standard procedures,
and operating guidelines and those formerly in place have become more
detailed. Administrators argue that knowing "what to do" and "how to do
it" is more complex. Many describe the myriad of rules and regulations
as "overwhelming" (Black-Branch, 1993a). There is no doubt that the
Charter has contributed to the erosion of traditional administrative
authority, particularly in regard to student discipline.

Whereas the legal doctrine of *in loco parentis* once granted
educators a wide range of authority to act in place of the parent, the
Charter now challenges this notion. The doctrine of *in loco parentis* is
defined as "in the place of a parent; instead of a parent; charged,
factitiously, with a parent's rights, duties and responsibilities (Black's Law
Dictionary, 1979, p. 708). This doctrine is listed under section 43 of the
Criminal Code. Section 43 states: "Every schoolteacher, parent or person
standing in the place of a parent is justified in using force by way of
correction toward a pupil or child, as the case may be, who is under his
care, if the force does not exceed what is reasonable under the

circumstances."[2] Legal rights provisions in the *Charter* undoubtedly change the traditional role of school principals, and teachers.

Legal Rights Provisions

Legal rights are defined under sections 7 to 14 in the *Charter*. The *Charter* specifically states:

7.   Everyone has the right to life, liberty and security of person and the right not to be deprived thereof except in accordance with the principles of fundamental justice.

8.   Everyone has the right to be secure against unreasonable search or seizure.

9.   Everyone has the right not to be arbitrarily detained or imprisoned.

10.   Everyone has the right on arrest or detention
(a) to be informed promptly of the reasons therefore;
(b) to retain and instruct counsel without delay and to be informed of that right; and
(c) to have the validity of the detention determined by way of *habeas corpus* and to be released if the detention is not lawful.

11.   Any person charged with an offence has the right
(a) to be informed without unreasonable delay of the specific offence;
(b) to be tried within a reasonable time;
(c) not to be compelled to be a witness in proceedings against that person in respect of the offence;
(d) to be presumed innocent until proven guilty according to law in a fair and public hearing by an independent and impartial tribunal;
(e) not to be denied reasonable bail without just cause;
(f) except in the case of an offence under military law tried before a military tribunal, to the benefit of trial by jury where the maximum punishment for the offence is

---

[2]   See: *Ogg-Moss v. R.* [1984] 2 S.C.R. 173, 111 D.L.R. (4th) 549 (S.C.C.).

imprisonment for five years or a more severe punishment;
(g) not to be found guilty on account of any act or omission unless, at the time of the act or omission, it constituted an offence under Canadian or international law or was criminal according to the general principles of law recognized by the community of nations;
(h) if finally acquitted of the offence, not to be tried for it again and, if finally found guilty and punished for the offence, not to be tried or punished for it again; and
(i) if found guilty of the offence and if the punishment for the offence has been varied between the time of commission and the time of sentencing, to the benefit of the lesser punishment.

12.   Everyone has the right not to be subjected to any cruel and unusual treatment or punishment.

13.   A witness who testifies in any proceedings has the right not to have any incriminating evidence so given used to incriminate that witness in any other proceedings, except in a prosecution for perjury or for the giving of contradictory evidence.

14.   A party or witness in any proceedings who does not understand or speak the language in which the proceedings are conducted or who is deaf has the right to the assistance of an interpreter.

Does the *Charter* Apply?

Following the enactment of the *Charter*, debate surfaced as to whether legal rights enshrined under constitutional law would actually affect education. Whilst some argued these rights were intended solely for criminal matters and would not impinge on day-to-day life in schools, others advocated a number of legal implications regarding administrative practices. To this day a court of law has yet to deal with the issue.

In the case of *R. v. G. (James Michael) (J. M. G.)* (1986), (which will be discussed further in this chapter) the judge raised this very issue and stated that he would "assume" the *Charter* applies to education. So whilst the issue as to whether the *Charter* actually applies to legal rights issues in education lingers, in the interim a number of important cases are being heard by the courts regarding education and legal rights provisions.

Legal Rights Case Law

A number of cases relating to legal rights and administrative practices have been challenged under the *Charter*. Recent *Charter* case law indicates that breaches of students' legal rights are fertile grounds for law suits. In these cases, it seems judges are upholding traditional administrative practices subordinating the legal rights of students to the reasonable management of schools.

Although many *Charter* cases in this area pertain to matters involving student discipline, other teacher and parent-related issues have also evolved. Cases discussed in this chapter involve issues of legal rights regarding: student rights, teacher rights, the application of the *Charter*, special education, and school closure as well as other issues as discussed throughout this chapter.

The Due Process of Law

Many legal rights cases within the educational context involve the right to "life, liberty and security of the person" under section 7. This provision is more commonly known as the "due process" clause. Examples of such were discussed in the previous chapter in the cases of *Kind* and *Cline* where the parents in both these cases successfully argued they had been denied the right to "life, liberty and security of the person" in keeping with the principles of "fundamental justice" under section 7 of the *Charter*. The courts in both these instances ruled that the denial of the plaintiffs' applications to home instruct their children were decided in an arbitrary fashion which effectively violated their right to due process. Other examples regarding due process will be discussed in this chapter and throughout this book.

Student Rights: Drugs, Search, Seizure and Detention

The case of *R. v. G. (James Michael)* (1986) involved a fourteen-year-old
Thunder Bay student. The school principal heard from a student that
James Michael was in possession of illegal drugs, which he had placed in
his socks. James Michael was summoned to the principal's office where
he was instructed to remove his shoes and socks. The principal himself
removed a piece of tinfoil (containing marijuana) from James Michael's
sock or pant leg (it was unclear which in the testimony). The police were
called and upon their arrival promptly arrested James Michael, informing
him of his *Charter* rights. James Michael was convicted under the *Young
Offenders Act* for possession of narcotics.

He claimed that his legal rights under section 10(a) of the *Charter*
had been violated by his being detained to be searched. He also claimed
that the school principal failed to inform him of his right to counsel before
asking him to remove his shoes and socks and therefore the drugs were
found during an illegal search.

The Ontario Court of Appeal decision was in favour of the school.
The Court did not, as a matter of *stare decisis,*[3] hold that the *Charter*
applied to the principal under these circumstances. It just "assumed" it
did. In effect, the Court did not have to decide the question since it found
no *Charter* violation. The Court concluded, however, that students are
subject to discipline by school authorities by virtue of their attending the
school. Commenting on the issue of the search and seizure the Court
stated that the distinction between the actual search of this student and
other disciplinary actions was the degree of potential "significant legal
consequences" for the student. The Court went on to say that the search
in this case was merely an extension of normal disciplinary actions.
School management includes reasonable disciplinary actions or
investigative procedures to assist in managing schools. The Court found
no evidence to suggest that the principal was doing anything other than
performing his duties as prescribed under the *Education Act*.[4]

---

3   Stare decisis is a latin term meaning: "to stand by things decided. . . .
precedent" (Oxford Concise Dictionary of Law, 1990).
4   An application for leave to appeal to the Supreme Court of Canada was dismissed
on 27 January 1987.

Legal Authority to Search Students

The *James Michael G.* case is an important decision for school administrators. Since the Court found legal authority for the principal to conduct a personal search in his statutory duty to ensure proper order and discipline (then section 236(a) -- now section 265(a)), in effect, the Court was legally characterizing the principal as an agent of the state.[5]

Mature Student: Drugs, Breach of Discipline and Detention

In *R. v. Sweet* (1986), a nineteen-year-old student was detained for what was described as a serious breach of school discipline. Several teachers alleged that Sweet had been smoking marijuana in school. Sweet was told to stand against the wall in the hallway, to await the arrival of the vice-principal. Sweet defied the order and left the school, physically assaulting a teacher who attempted to keep him from leaving. Charged with assault, Sweet claimed his *Charter* rights were violated in three ways. First, he contended that he was arbitrarily detained (section 9), second, he was denied the principles of fundamental justice under section 7 of the *Charter* and, third, he was not promptly informed as to why he was detained (section 10(a)).

The Court looked to the *R. v. J. M. G.* case in reaching its decision. It stated that these legal rights, within the meaning of section 10(a), do not apply in a situation of an alleged serious breach of school discipline. In fact, it concluded that had the principal and teachers not acted in this situation, it would have been a serious dereliction of their duties. Since such a detention did not constitute a detention within the meaning of section 10 of the *Charter*, the teachers were under no duty to inform the student of the reasons for his being ordered to stay. Moreover, he had not been arbitrarily detained under section 9. The Court also found no evidence that the principles of fundamental justice, under section 7 of the *Charter*, had been violated.

---

[5]   For further discussion on the *J. M. G.* case see: Black-Branch, J. L. (1994a) Weighing the Balance Between Constitutional Legal Rights and Administrative Duties. *The Canadian Administrator, Vol. 33, No. 8, May.*

Student Rights: Drugs, Search, Seizure and Reasonableness

R. v. W. and B. (1990) involved an incident of search and seizure under section 8 of the *Charter*.   Two young offenders were charged with possession of narcotics found in their lockers.   They were initially acquitted by a Provincial Court.   The Court ruled that the evidence (the narcotics) was obtained during an illegal search by the school principal and therefore the evidence was inadmissible in Court.   Hence, there was no evidence on which to convict the two students.

The Supreme Court of Newfoundland, however, reversed the acquittal.   The Court stated that it is not unreasonable for a principal to search a student's locker.   School locker searches are "not excessively intrusive" and "do not require prior police authorization", particularly when a principal has to act hastily.   Because the search did not contravene *Charter* provisions under section 8 (search or seizure), the application to exclude the evidence, under section 24(2) of the *Charter*, was rejected. The evidence was used in court and the two students were convicted of possession of drugs.

Student Rights: Drugs, Illegal Seizure and Detention

In another case involving drugs, *R. v. J. R. G.* (1991) a British Columbia Youth Court heard a case regarding an alleged unlawful detention.   In this case a school counsellor received a call from a parent indicating that a student was in possession of narcotics.   The student was removed from class and not permitted to use the washroom.

The student was advised to speak to the school counsellor -- who was described as being trustworthy.   The student was not advised of his right to legal counsel.   In fact, the counsellor advised the student that it would be easier for all involved if he were to reveal any drugs he had. The student then produced a cigarette package in which there were drugs. The police were contacted and the student was subsequently charged with possession of marijuana.

Under these circumstances the Youth Court upheld the student's *Charter* argument that he had been illegally detained under section 10(b) of the *Charter*.   The Court decided that, in this particular case, the school encouraged the student's co-operation, not fully explaining the jeopardy involved in his co-operation.   The counsellor (a person who could be trusted) convinced the student to admit to having drugs in his possession under uncertain pretences, whilst a police officer might not have had reasonable and probable grounds to conduct a search.   The Court ruled that the evidence was to be excluded from the trial because it might not have been otherwise obtained had the school not intervened.

Student Rights: Expulsion and the Presumption of Innocence

In the case of *Peel Board of Education v. B. (W.)* (1990),[6] the Ontario Supreme Court ruled that technically speaking, section 11 of the *Charter*, regarding the presumption of innocence until proven guilty, would not apply in non-criminal proceedings. In this case, some students allegedly kidnapped and sexually assaulted a female student. The Court ordered that the school was not to hold an expulsion hearing for the students accused of kidnapping and sexual assault. It felt that such a hearing would reveal the identities of the accused, which is contrary to the *Young Offenders Act*. This case raises questions concerning the degree to which a young offender's confidentiality will be upheld and suggests that protection of the rights of an accused in a criminal proceeding will be superior to school authority when the *Young Offenders Act* is involved.[7]

Student Rights: Self-Incriminating Statements and the Right to Consultation

In the case of *R. v. B. C. W.* (1986) a fifteen-year-old student faced criminal charges regarding the starting of a fire in a Manitoba high school.

[6]   The case originated as *Re: Peel Board of Education and B et al.* (1987), heard by the High Court of Ontario.

[7]   It should be noted that there is some confusion and ambivalence amongst many administrators and teachers as to the actual difference between the *Young Offenders Act* and the *Canadian Charter of Rights and Freedoms*, the former being a federal act and the latter constitutional law.   For further discussion on this difference and the perceptions of educators in this regard see Black-Branch (1993a) *Traditions Rights and Realities: Legal,* de facto *and Symbolic Influences of the* Canadian Charter of Rights and Freedoms *on Educational Administration in Canada.*

During a police interrogation, the student made self-incriminating statements. The police then charged, cautioned and informed the student of his rights under the *Charter*. At that time he also signed a waiver of his rights under section 56 of the *Young Offenders Act*.

In spite of the waiver, the Manitoba Court of Appeal held that the student's statements were inadmissible. The police did not explain the right to consultation to him. The Act requires that a young person must have an opportunity to consult an adult as soon as a police officer has a reasonable opportunity to comply with section 56(2). In this case, the police did not ask the accused if he wished to see his mother who was at the police station during his interrogation. It did not matter that the mother had chosen not to see her son upon learning of his interrogation. The self-incriminating statements were not admissible.

Participation in Sports and Board Prescribed Eligibility Requirements

In *Warkentin et al. v. Sault Ste. Marie Board of Education et al.,* two nineteen-year-old high school students in northern Ontario challenged an athletics eligibility requirement stating that: "no student could compete in any sport for more than 10 consecutive semesters". Enrolled in Grade 13 for the second time to complete certain course credits, both students had played for the school's senior basketball team for the prescribed period and wished to do so again. The purpose of the eligibility provision was to ensure that students who failed to meet minimum academic requirements would devote their full time to academic endeavours and not return to school solely for sports. The students requested an injunction against the eligibility requirement.

The District Court refused to grant the injunction they requested to restrain the association of secondary schools from interfering with their right to play basketball. The Court found that the association had passed the ineligibility rule for a *bona fide* purpose and had the power and authority to make it part of its constitution. There was no violation of section 7 of the *Charter* because the students' liberty was not affected. Although the School Board had passed a resolution suspending applicability of the eligibility rule and then some weeks later rescinded its own resolution, the Court held that the Board had exercised its powers in a valid manner. There was no evidence of bad faith which would have entitled the Court to challenge the Board's decision.

Élitist Tendencies in Judicial Rulings: Discipline and Control Over Students

The above cases focused predominantly on the constitutional rights of students. It would seem that the judiciary is willing to uphold traditional practices whereby administrators and teachers alike have control over students within educational institutions. Courts will only rule against the actions of administrators when it is felt that they have acted in an excessive and unreasonable manner, such as deliberately misleading a student to believe something other than the truth, as in the case of *R. v. J. R. G.*, or by denying them their rights in accordance with the *Young Offenders Act*.

Nevertheless, the precedent set in the *James Michael G.* case sends a clear message to school principals that they are to conduct business as normal within schools. They are to take control for the reasonable well-being of the wider school community. The follow-up case of *Sweet* indicates that educators are not only encouraged to do so, they are indeed compelled to act in situations of a breach of discipline. To not do so would amount to a breach of their statutory duties pursuant to the *Education Act*. This reiterates the notion that regardless of the *Charter*, the courts support the political *status quo*, in so far as administrators must maintain a safe and secure educational environment.

The judiciary is only willing to rule against the system when there has been an apparent abuse of administrative authority which cannot be tempered by the limitations clause, under section 1. What is more, the case of *Warkentin* indicates that schools retain the power to set policies which they see fit for the reasonable education of the young. See also the *Devereux* case in the previous chapter regarding school policies on dress codes.

Subpoenaing a Pupil's Records with Certainty

The case of *R. v. Nelson* (1989) illustrates that courts can intervene in school and private matters as the judiciary deems appropriate. During a trial where a teacher was faced with charges of sexual touching and sexual assault, the High Court of Ontario allowed the defence to subpoena a pupil's records, without a hearing to do so. It must be noted that the Court wanted access to specific information that would be provided in the file.

Subpoenaing a Pupil's Records with No Certainty

In the case of *Desmarais v. Morrissette* (1991), however, the court quashed a subpoena *ducas tecum* obtained by Morrissette for the purposes of defending previous charges of sexual assault. Morrissette was hoping to find evidence in his file which was compiled by the Ottawa Board of Education psychologist (Desmarais). Morrissette claimed it was his right under sections 7 and 11(d) of the *Charter* to have access to the file. He felt it might provide evidence that would support his case against allegations of sexual assault.

The Court stated that Morrissette's request amounted to that of a fishing expedition. A file of this nature should not be at "the beck and call" of an accused. The Court dismissed the *Charter* arguments and quashed the subpoena. It held that it is in the interests of the Ottawa Board of Education, and others, that privilege be granted to the working notes of the psychologists.

Subpoenaing a Pupil's Records: Certainty versus Non-Certainty

It must be noted that in the case of *Nelson*, the court wanted access to specific information. In *Desmarais*, however, there was no certainty that the alleged information would be found in the student's record. That being so, the main difference between these two cases is that Morrissette wanted access to the files for what would amount to a "fishing expedition", whereas in *Nelson* there appeared to be substantive evidence which was vital to the case at hand. It would appear that courts are willing to support the subpoenaing of a student's record if there is a high degree of certainty that the information sought after is indeed present, and of course, relevant to the case at hand. It also indicates that each case will be decided on the balance of its individual merits on a case-by-case basis.

Teacher Rights: Suspension Without Pay

Legal rights cases affect more than students. A case involving a teacher occurred in *Noyes v. Board of School Trustees, District No. 30 (South Cariboo)* (1985). Noyes was suspended from his teaching duties, without pay, as a result of criminal charges brought against him. He claimed his legal rights under section 7, life, liberty and security of person, and section 11(d), to be presumed innocent until proven guilty according to law in a fair and public hearing by an independent and impartial tribunal, had been violated.

The Supreme Court of British Columbia could not find any way in which Noyes' section 7 rights had been violated. His rights to life, liberty and security of person had not been threatened or jeopardized. Secondly, section 122(1)(b) of the British Columbia *School Act*, regarding suspension, did not contravene section 11(d) (presumed innocent until proven guilty) because the provisions in the *School Act* did not presume he was guilty.

In addition, Noyes claimed discrimination under section 15(1), equality before and under the law and equal protection and benefit of law. He argued that not receiving pay whilst suspended was discriminatory. The Court could not determine, and it did not wish to "speculate", whether the School Board had committed a procedural error in not granting Noyes pay whilst suspended. Therefore, since no apparent *Charter* right had been violated, the Court could not offer any remedy under section 24(1) of the *Charter*. All *Charter* arguments were rejected and Noyes' case was dismissed.

Teacher Rights: Sexual Assault and Reasonable Doubt

A fourteen-year-old female student claimed her social studies teacher had placed a hand on her shoulder, then moved it to her left breast, whilst helping her with her school work. The Newfoundland teacher denied the incident. The police subsequently charged the social studies teacher with sexual assault under section 246.1(1) of the *Criminal Code*.

In the case of *R. v. Boone* (1989) the Newfoundland Provincial
Court examined whether the Crown had proven the teacher's guilt beyond
a reasonable doubt. After considering the incident in what was described
as "through the eyes of an objective observer", the Court dismissed the
charge of sexual assault. It found no evidence of motive on the teacher's
part and noted inconsistencies in the student's testimony. The evidence
thus fell far short of the "beyond a reasonable doubt" standard.

Teacher Rights: Gross Indecency

A British Columbia trial court convicted a teacher of the offence of gross
indecency committed against a Grade 6 male student during the period
from September, 1972 to October, 1973. In the case of *R. v. Stymiest*
(1993), the teacher appealed against his conviction on five grounds and
lost on all of them: (1) Although 14 months and 24 days from the date of
the charge to the conclusion of the trial had elapsed, the teacher could not
prove that his section 11(b) *Charter* rights to be tried within a reasonable
time had been violated; (2) The teacher could not prove that his sections 7
and 11(d) *Charter* rights had been violated as a result of the pre-charge
delay (in excess of seventeen years) in bringing the matter to trial;   (3)
The teacher could not prove that the jury's verdict was unreasonable or
unsupported by the evidence; (4) The teacher could not prove that his
right to a fair trial was prejudiced by the inflammatory and unfair
statements of the Crown counsel to the jury in her closing remarks; and,
(5) The teacher could not prove that the trial judge erred by failing to
properly instruct the jury about the need for corroboration of the former
student's allegations.

Application of the *Charter* to Statutory Bodies

The case of *Weinstein et al. v. Ministry of Education for British Columbia
et al.* [1985] involved both issues of liberty and security of the person and
section 15(1), equality rights.   This particular case dealt with the
applicability of the *Charter* with regards to provincial legislation.   The
Lieutenant Governor-in-Council of British Columbia removed the
Vancouver School Trustees, a statutory body, for failing to approve a

budget within the guidelines set out in section 12(1) of the *Education (Interim) Finance Act.* The Supreme Court of British Columbia ruled that the actions taken by the Lieutenant Governor-in-Council, pursuant to section 15(i) of the *School Act* violated neither section 7 nor section 15(1) of the *Charter.* The Court stated that rights and freedoms under the *Charter* are guaranteed to individuals and not to statutory bodies.

Application of the *Charter* to Teacher Federations

In *Tomen et al. v. Federation of Women Teachers' Associations of Ontario* (1989), Tomen sought a court declaration to strike down section 2(a) of By-law 1 of the Ontario Teachers' Federation as unconstitutional. Section 2(a) stated that women teaching all, or most, of their assigned teaching duties in an elementary school must belong to the Federation of Women Teachers. The Court upheld the validity of this by-law.

The Court also ruled that the by-law was not a regulation approved by the Lieutenant Governor-in-Council, and therefore was not a "governmental matter" but rather a rule that regulates members of a private organization. As such, it was not governed by section 32(1) of the *Charter.*[8]

The Constitutionality of the Alberta School Act

In the case of *Jacobi v. Newell No. 4 (County) et al.* (1992), an Alberta family decided to sue several school boards and a county by seeking a declaration that certain provisions of the *School Act* were inconsistent with section 2(a) and section 15 of the *Charter* and section 1(b) and (c) of the Alberta *Bill of Rights.* The school boards and county applied to the Court of Queen's Bench to halt the family's action or to transfer the proceedings to another judicial district and to require the family to provide security for costs.

The Court dismissed the application to strike the proceedings even though the family no longer resided in Alberta. It did, however, transfer the action and ordered the family to provide security. Since this case dealt

---

[8]   In *Tomen*, leave to appeal to the Supreme Court of Canada was refused.

primarily with procedural matters, there was no discussion of the substantive issues.

In the subsequent case of *Jacobi v. Board of Education of Aqueduct Roman Catholic Separate School District No. 37* (1994) the Alberta Court of Queen's Bench ruled that the Aqueduct Roman Catholic Separate School Board was without status to act as a separate school board. As a result, the parents did not have to direct their property taxes thereto, nor were they required to send their children to these separate schools.

Legal Rights, Special Education and Enrolment

In the cases of *Re: Maw et al. and Board of Education for the Borough of Scarborough et al.* (1983) and *Bales v. Board of School Trustees (Central Okanagan)* (1984), the plaintiffs argued violations of special education students' rights under section 7, life, liberty and security of person. In the case of *Re: Maw*, three parents had requested the Boards of Education in Scarborough and Etobicoke (two in Etobicoke and one in Scarborough), to hold a "hard to serve pupil" hearing for their "exceptional" children. This type of hearing for exceptional children is required under the *Education Act*. At the time of the request, however, the students were not registered in the respective School Boards. The Boards stated that they were required to hold "hard to serve pupil" hearings for only the pupils registered in their boards. Hence, the Boards of Education dismissed the parents' requests.

The parents requested the Court quash the Boards' decisions not to hold a "hard to serve pupil" hearing, pursuant to section 34(2) of the Ontario *Education Act*. They claimed the Boards' decisions violated their *Charter* rights under section 7. The Ontario High Court of Justice ruled that the plaintiffs were not denied their section 7 rights. The Court found that the School Boards were justified in not permitting the parents to have access to a "hard to serve pupil" hearing because the children were not registered in the School Boards.

The Court stated that "We are of the view that the right to liberty referred to in s[ection] 7 of the Canadian *Charter of Rights and Freedoms*, is not infringed by the requirement of enrolment in a school operated by the respondent Board" (43 O.R. (2d), 1983, p. 698). In other words,

Boards of Education are not required to hold a "hard to serve pupil" hearing if the children in question are not "pupils" enrolled in their Board. The application to quash the Boards' decisions was thus dismissed.

Legal Rights, Special Education and Mainstreaming

In *Bales* the parents wanted their child to attend regular classes. The child, who had suffered brain dysfunction as an infant, had attended a regular school and was transferred to a school for the "moderately handicapped", against the wishes of the parents. According to the British Columbia *School Act,* the administration had the authority to assign students to the classes, or schools, they deemed appropriate. The parents argued against this authority on section 7 grounds.

The Court action was dismissed. The judge found no evidence that the principles of fundamental justice had been denied as there was no deprivation of life, liberty or security of the person. The Court stated it was not for the courts to decide whether the child should receive the "benefits which integration is thought to provide". Specifically, the Court spoke to this argument with regard to the alleged discrimination.

> In so far as special education involves discrimination between handicapped and non-handicapped, the distinction is drawn for the purpose of providing the handicapped with the special treatment they require. Where, as here, the segregation involved is reasonably directed to the achievement of that objective -- even though it may exceed the degree of segregation now considered by experts to be strictly necessary -- it cannot be characterized as discrimination in an objectionable sense, nor as a breach of any other guarantee or commitment contained in the enactments and conventions cited by the plaintiffs. (54 B.C.L.R., p. 203)

It should be noted that this is an early decision and the courts were apprehensive about issuing rulings regarding special education. Judicial reluctance of this nature slowly changed, as discussed later in this chapter (see *Trofimenkoff*) and in the next chapter in the cases dealing with equality rights and special education.

School Closure, Due Process and Judicial Review

In *Hardy v. Minister of Education*, (1985), Madam Justice McLachlin quashed the British Columbia Minister of Education's order to close a school. The judge ruled in favour of the community's claim that their rights to fundamental justice had been violated because they had not been given adequate notice of the pending school closure. In addition, the community was not provided an adequate forum to express their views on the Board's decision to close the school.

The judge's decision clearly upheld the principles of fundamental justice, at that time rejecting precedent in Ontario cases that school administrative actions of this nature are not subject to judicial review. More recent Ontario rulings, however, indicate that school administrative actions are subject to judicial review.

Application of the *Charter* Regarding School Closure and Reduced Staff

In the case of *Ignatescu v. Board of Education of Assiniboia School Division No. 69* the Court of the Queen's Bench ruled that the *Charter* did not apply in the instance where the Board resolved to reduce the number of staff at two schools. The plaintiff claimed that this decision denied principles of fundamental justice under section 7. The court ruled that the Board was not exercising a quasi-judicial function in reaching its decision and therefore the application for *certiorari* to quash the decision was not accorded.

School for the Deaf: Closure and Equality

In another *Charter*-related case of a school closing, *Trofimenkoff v. Meiklejohn* (1991), section 7 and section 15 *Charter* arguments were rejected, upholding the Saskatchewan Ministry's decision to close a school for the hearing impaired. In this case, the school had been administered by the province from 1981-91. Student enrolment had decreased from 113 to 34 students. Following an investigation and the submission of a report by a special task force in June 1990, the Province announced that it would close the R. J. D. Williams Provincial School for the Deaf in Saskatoon, Saskatchewan.

The plaintiffs (parents, students and teachers) alleged, *inter alia*, discrimination and the violation of legal rights. They claimed that the *Charter* required the province to make special provisions for special education students and it had failed in its responsibility to do so. Specifically, they claimed that the provisions of the *Education Act* or the *Education Regulations 1986* discriminated against disabled students thus violating their rights under section 15(1) of the *Charter*. They also alleged a denial of legal rights of fundamental justice as guaranteed under section 7 of the *Charter*.

The plaintiffs argued that the students at the Williams school would be denied an education upon closing the school because the Minister of Education and the Government of Saskatchewan did not possess "an adequate understanding of the issues in deaf education". In addition, "indiscriminate mainstreaming of deaf students is not in their best interests". They felt that these factors inadvertently denied deaf students their right to an education which is an embodied right under section 7, according to the Supreme Court of Canada ruling in *R. v. Jones*. Furthermore, the plaintiffs were not given an adequate opportunity "to defend their interest".

The Court of the Queen's Bench dismissed these and other arguments saying there was no evidence that the Ministry had failed in its duty to provide special educational provisions for these students. The students were being accommodated at other educational institutions.

On appeal to the Saskatchewan Court of Appeal in *Trofimenkoff v. Saskatchewan Minister of Education* (1991), the appellants sought interim and permanent injunctive relief requiring the Minister of Education and the Government of Saskatchewan to meet their legal obligations to deaf students. In particular, they sought, *inter alia*, a declaration that the announced closure of the R. J. D. Williams School was "unlawful" and that the Minister of Education and the Government of Saskatchewan were obligated "to keep open and operating" the R. J. D. Williams Provincial School for the Deaf.

The Court dismissed the appeal. It stated that "the wisdom of the policy [decision] and the substance of it are matters for the Minister, who is responsible to the Legislature, members of whom are of course ultimately responsible to the electorate" (97 Sask. R. p. 163). The court instructed the appellants that theirs is a "narrow legal" function aimed at considering the "legality, or lack thereof, of the Minister's actions". They were not in a place to weigh the merits of integrated or segregated educational systems.[9]

Élitist Tendencies in Judicial Rulings: Integration and Mainstreaming

The decisions in the *Trofimenkoff* cases, both at the Court of the Queen's Bench and at the Court of Appeal level, seem to support the popular political ideology of integrating deaf special needs children into mainstream settings. Once again, this supports the argument that the courts tend to support political ideology over an independent assessment based on the actual facts and the merits of each individual case.

Whilst there may not have been procedural errors in the ruling of the Court of the Queen's Bench *per se*, it could be argued that the issues were not considered thoroughly in regard to notions of equality and legal rights, hence the interim order should have been granted until the matter was dealt with properly. Whilst it may be true that the Court of Appeal, in particular, is not faced with the task of weighing the merits of a case in making a decision regarding interim relief, it is also true that it should issue the order if there is a chance that irreparable harm may ensue in the event of the order not being issued before the merits of the case are properly weighed. However, the Court opted to err on the side of caution and support the political views of the elected Minister of Education over the principles of enshrined rights and freedoms.

The Court stated clearly that the "substance" of the policy decision is for the Minister ("who is responsible to the Legislature, members of whom are of course ultimately responsible to the electorate") to decide. One could argue that this notion defeats the purpose of entrenching rights under a constitution if indeed the courts are willing to bow to the supremacy of provincial legislatures and not rule on these issues in accordance with their new judicial role behaviour.

There is a distinct departure from the *Bales* case discussed earlier

---

9   For further discussion on the *Trofimenkoff* case see: Black-Branch, J. L. (1994b) Fallen on Deaf Ears: A Legal Analysis of the Closure of the R. J. D. Williams Provincial School for the Deaf. *ACEHI Journal, Vol. 20, Issue 1/2.*

whereby the judge was apprehensive about ruling in matters of special education. It would seem that by this time, some ten years later, the courts were more likely to rule on these issues. In addition, it should be noted that the political *status quo* was supported in both cases. At the time of *Bales*, it was proper to uphold the position of the school (that of educators), and the popularity of mainstreaming was not as widespread. Today, the concept of mainstreaming has become quite popular and is favoured by politicians, as evidenced by the *Trofimenkoff* case in Saskatchewan.

Legal Rights Practical Applications

It is, of course, impossible to predict how judges will rule in the future. Each case is unique and contextual to the given circumstances. Nevertheless, there are a number of suggestions for administrators and teachers alike. In regard to student discipline, the all-important word in these circumstance is "reasonable". The judiciary appear likely to rule in favour of the school when educators act in a reasonable fashion for the safety, security and general well-being of the school community. It is only in extreme situations where the courts are more likely to rule against educational authority.

Searching a student's locker for illegal drugs may well be within the scope of educational duty, providing the student has had the opportunity to participate in the process and understand the importance of the situation. A court is not likely to support actions that mislead a student to believe "all will be fine" when, in fact, legal implications are imminent. In addition, the cases illustrate that educators are indeed obliged to maintain order and discipline within schools. Teachers failing to exercise their statutory duties may be held in breach of their responsibility, as prescribed under the *Education Act*.

Decisions on issues involving teachers, parents and those of a more technical administrative nature are likely to be based on whether there have been procedural errors and not necessarily on the merits of the case *per se*, unless there is an apparent political reason to do so. Courts are likely to stick to the facts and ensure that all legalities have been adhered to, be it in regard to school closure or the issuing of injunctions to prevent certain actions. Whilst the question remains as to whether the

Charter actually applies within the educational context, in relation to legal rights, it is best to "assume" it does.   Although the courts are apprehensive to deal with the issue head-on in cases involving disciplinary actions (such as in the case of *James Michael G.*), they seem quick to say when the *Charter* does not apply in regard to administrative powers (see *Weinstein* and *Tomen*).

5 Equality Rights

Introduction

Academics, educators and practitioners feel that equality rights provisions under section 15 of the *Charter* opens the way for a multitude of changes within school systems. Most agree that inequitable practices will be more susceptible than ever to legal scrutiny. Claims of discrimination and inequitable treatment will not only become more prevalent but they will be taken more seriously than in the past.

Essentially the equality rights provision has two main sections: section 15(1) which provides for anti-discrimination and section 15(2) which is an affirmative action provision. Section 15 specifically states:

15(1)   Every individual is equal before and under the law and has the right to the equal protection and equal benefit of the law without discrimination and, in particular, without discrimination based on race, national or ethnic origin, colour, religion, sex, age or mental or physical disability.

15(2)   Subsection (1) does not preclude any law, program or activity that has as its object the amelioration of conditions of disadvantaged individuals or groups including those that are disadvantaged because of race, national or ethnic origin, colour, religion, sex, age or mental or physical disability.

Each of these sections, and their respective legal implications for education will be discussed in turn, followed by the case law in the area of equality rights.

The Guarantees of Equality

At first sight the guarantees of equality under section 15(1) may seem somewhat repetitive. The section provides that every individual shall be "equal before and under the law and has the right to the equal protection and equal benefit of the law". But in reality, the wording of this clause was well thought through. Specifically, section 15(1) makes four categorical distinctions in the concept of equity: (1) "equality before the law" was directly transferred from the *Canadian Bill of Rights* so as to maintain existing equality rights; (2) "equality under the law" means that one can legally challenge both the application and the content of law; (3) "equal protection of the law" is the wording in the U.S. Fourteenth Amendment so American comparisons can be drawn and American jurisprudence used to argue cases; and, (4) "equal benefit of the law" is included so as not to advantage some individuals over others.

The fine tuning of these distinctions, which may at first seem irrelevant to most, seeks to address what lobby groups, particularly those representing the interests of women, saw as possible loopholes in guaranteeing equality rights. The important point is that much care and scrutiny went into the drafting of this section so as to ensure the highest possible guarantee of equity under the *Charter*.

Horizontal Equity and Non-Preferential Treatment

Essentially, section 15(1) promotes what may be called "horizontal equity" or, the equal treatment of supposed equals. Specifically intended to prevent discrimination against specific classes and groups of people, as well as individuals, these guarantees have many legal implications for Canadian schools. For example, in schools the *Charter* aims to ward off discrimination in the form of preferential treatment to one particular ethnicity or racial origin over another. It also seeks to protect against discrimination based on mental or physical disability. It seeks to prevent discrimination based on gender. In other words, section 15(1) promotes horizontal equity in that all people are to be treated equally, regardless of, *inter alia*, gender, ability or ethnic background. It promotes the equal treatment of supposed equals. It presumes that all people are equal.

Affirmative Action: Vertical Equity and Preferential Treatment

The aim of section 15(2) of the *Canadian Charter of Rights and Freedoms* is to "ameliorate" the conditions of those who have been traditionally disadvantaged on the grounds of gender or ethnicity. This provision allows school systems the opportunity to implement affirmative action programmes which, in essence, advantage women, visible minorities, aboriginal peoples, and the disabled, whilst legally discriminating against other groups and individuals (i.e., Caucasian males). Thus, the intent of affirmative action (often referred to as positive or reverse discrimination) goes beyond providing horizontal equity, the equal treatment of presumed equals. It allows for vertical equity, the differential or preferential treatment of people who are in different circumstances.

Affirmative Action and Employment Equity

The federal and provincial governments actively encourage affirmative action programmes in accordance with the *Employment Equity Act 1986*. In fact, women, minorities, aboriginal peoples, as well as the disabled, have been identified by the federal Government as target groups for achieving employment equity. Government, under the *Employment Equity Act 1986*, actively encourages employers to institute affirmative action programmes by offering special grants and tax incentives for those who do so. In other words, affirmative action programmes are legal under constitutional law. What is more, they are politically encouraged under legislation. Their success depends largely on those implementing them at the grassroots level.

Affirmative Action in Ontario

The Government of the Province of Ontario provides one of numerous examples of changes that came about as a result of the *Charter*. The Ontario Ministry of Education began after 1985 (the year the equality section (section 15) came into force) to work towards affirmative action for women in the area of educational administration, for example. The following schedule of events supports this contention:

1985:   The Ontario Ministry of Education provided an incentive fund for boards to support and implement employment equity and the Ministry's Policy/Program Memo 92 established goal of 30% women in all educational occupational categories by the year 2000.

1989:   Bill 69 (amendment to the *Education Act*) gave the Ministry of Education authority to order boards to establish and maintain affirmative action regarding the employment of women.

1990:   Ministry of Education Policy/Program Memo 111 mandated 50% women in all positions of responsibility by the year 2000.

1991:   Bill 125 -- employment equity expanded to visible minorities.

It should be noted that these *de facto*[1] policy changes all happened within the first five to six years after section 15 of the *Charter* came into force.

Affirmative Action in School Boards

Today, most school systems have enacted affirmative action policies of some sort or another. They encourage gender and racial equity through affirmative action in order to increase the numbers of women and visible minorities both in teaching positions within the school system at large and in positions of added responsibility. For example, many boards of education currently advertise in their employment listings that they are "equal opportunity employers" and are "committed to employment equity". Some advertisements actually "encourage qualified female candidates to apply", or those of "minority or aboriginal backgrounds".

---

[1]   The author contends that there are three possible causes of educational change under the *Charter*, namely: (1) legal change;   (2) symbolic change;   and, (3) *de facto* change. (For further discussion on these classifications refer to Appendix III.)

Issues of equality and affirmative action are not so clear cut, however. Many of these programmes have created bitterness and resentment within the educational sector. Some experts fear a backlash. Whilst it is beyond the intent of this discussion to weigh the merits of affirmative action, the issues are raised simply because it is an important area of law in relation to the *Charter*, although no cases of any significance have come forth in this area to date.

Backlash Against Affirmative Action

Needless to say affirmative action has created a marked discomfort amongst many people. There is growing division amongst those wanting promotion. Males typically feel disenfranchized by female applicants. They fear that the notion of the proverbial "glass ceiling" has transformed into what the author calls the "male-box phenomenon" whereby males feel boxed into their current positions from which they are unlikely to move in terms of promotional opportunities.

Further, Caucasian females feel increasingly disenfranchized by females representing visible minorities. Just when they feel they are breaking through the "glass ceiling", they have hit what might be called the "white cloud syndrome" whereby their future is somewhat foggy in terms of their promotional opportunities. By hiring minority females instead of Caucasian, boards of education interested in promoting affirmative action hit two check-off points on the target group check list, namely: female and minority, instead of just that of female. Hence, in terms of numbers and statistical data, they have higher numbers in two categories of the target groups and thus appear to be more dedicated to affirmative action initatives.

Moreover, the notion of hiring and promoting visible minorities is not so clear cut. There is some friction between minority communities as various minority groups vie for positions. For example, those of Asian background are competing against blacks, latinos, aboriginal peoples, and so forth. As well, it would be naive to think that any of these communities is united entirely. There are splintered factions within, thus contributing to in-fighting within individual minority groups. In regard to the Black community, for example, there are those of Caribbean extraction and those from African countries, not to mention those who have been in North America for many generations and do not consider themselves either Caribbean or African.

Similarly, Asians are also divided in terms of those who are Chinese, Korean, Vietnamese, Pakistani, Bangladeshi, Sri Lankan, and Indian, to name but a few divisions. And even within such distinctive groups there are those who are divided on political issues. Then there is the religious question. Within various groups (be they minority or majority) there are those who claim minority status on religious grounds. Here again there is division.[2]

Affirmative Action: Inter-Conflict and Intra-Conflict

It would seem that problems created by affirmative action are much broader than simply the notion of hiring females over males. There is inter-conflict, that is conflict between genders and races in regard to affirmative action, and there is also intra-conflict, that is conflict amongst genders and races, regarding affirmative action programmes. That is to say, there is conflict between, and indeed amongst, females and males alike. And there is conflict between, and amongst, those of racial and religious minority groups. It is no longer simply a matter of some males feeling disenfranchized by females and some racial groups feeling disenfranchized by others.

Affirmative Action and the Certified Ghetto Syndrome

Furthermore, many would argue that affirmative action initiatives are also creating a ghetto mentality amongst some in educational systems and in

---

2   Even within broad religious groups there are both minor and major differences. Dutch Reformed Christians may have different views from Roman Catholics, Greek Orthodox Catholics or Protestants. Similarly, Jews of different religious backgrounds, Reformed, Conservative or Orthodox, have competing views. Those believing in Islam also have different views. That is to say, although many Shia Muslims take similar stands on a number of issues, different sects such as the Druz, the Twelves, the Zaydis and the Ismailis do not agree on all issues. Similarly, the Sunni Muslim sects, including the Malikis, the Shafais and the Hanafi, advance different points of view.

society at large. Talk is rife that particular candidates have been hired, or awarded positions of responsibility, by virtue of their gender, or perhaps their race, instead of their ability, training and experience. This phenomenon the author refers to as the certified ghetto syndrome whereby many highly qualified candidates are stigmatized by their gender or race, hence bearing the brunt of negative stereotypes within their profession, even though they may be the best candidate for a given position. Such a syndrome calls for measures of accountability to exonerate school systems of such accusations.

The Legality of Affirmative Action and Educational Accountability

Despite apparent disenchantment with such programmes, affirmative action is legal under section 15(2) of the *Charter*.[3] But regardless of this fact, it seems that there is a growing concern in many circles that there may be a backlash through civil disobedience (from teachers and parents alike) to force governments to slow the pace of trying to fill quotas.[4] This is of particular importance to school administrators who need student numbers to fill classes.

Without clear benchmarks of accountability, many informed people fear that parents may remove their children from schools, opting for private education, or indeed home instruction, because of their concern about standards, or perhaps their general disenchantment with a system in turmoil. Others argue, however, that despite some teething pain,

---

[3]   On 17 October 1995, the European Court of Justice issued a landmark ruling against the setting of affirmative action quotas in areas where women account for less than 50% of the workforce. In particular, the Court struck down a German law in the state of Breman which mandated a result of 50-50 job parity between men and women. At present, the 1976 European Union directive on equal rights allows governments to promote affirmative action thus violating the principle of equality between men and women when the aim is to remove "inequalities that effect women's opportunities". The Court stated that the German law setting a 50-50 mandate exceeded the intent of the affirmative action clause. Although this decision is not binding on Canadian courts, applying only to the fifteen member states of the European Union, it is an important international ruling regarding the legality of affirmative action programmes.

[4]   Ontario has recently announced plans to reserve a specified percentage of places (i.e., quotas) for visible minorities in teacher education programmes.

affirmative action is a necessary transition which will inevitably work its way through and make for a better educational system.[5]

The Ambiguous Nature of Equality under the *Charter*

Although it is an important component of the equality rights provisions under the *Charter*, affirmative action is not the only issue raised in that regard. In fact, many cases have come forward dealing with a variety of other issues. The problem stems from the actual wording of the *Charter* itself. Although the wording of section 15 is quite clear in its intent to promote equity, it is very broad in scope and not clear in its definition as to what actually constitutes equality.   Hence, it has far-reaching implications for education in many areas. Section 15 is arguably one of the most open-ended provisions enlisted in the *Charter*, leaving it open to judicial interpretation. It is arguably one of the most contentious because it is the fruit of strong lobby efforts by a variety of political interest groups.[6]

Section 15(1) seeks to eliminate discrimination based on the above mentioned criteria, namely: "race, national or ethnic origin, colour, religion, sex, age or mental or physical disability". Whilst these areas of possible discrimination are listed, others are implied but not listed *per se*. The inclusion of the phrase "in particular" in reference to discrimination indicates that the list is not exhaustive and does not preclude other forms of discrimination.

Questions arise as to which other areas are protected under section 15.   Is sexual orientation included, for example?   What about discrimination based on marital status? There is little doubt that questions of equality are neither easily defined nor resolved. The following body of case law will assist in clarifying some of the issues raised regarding equality rights and how judges are ruling in these areas. Provided first is the judicial interpretation of discrimination under the *Charter*.

---

5   The U.N. *Convention on Racial Discrimination* endorses the institution of affirmative action initiatives providing they are of a temporary nature and are instituted as a remedial measure to reverse past trends.

6   In particular, groups representing the interests of women played an instrumental role in the shaping of section 15.

Discrimination

Mr. Justice McIntyre defined the issue of discrimination in the case of *Andrews v. Law Society of British Columbia* [1989]. He states:

> I would say then that discrimination may be described as a distinction, whether intentional or not but based on grounds relating to personal characteristics of the individual or group, which has the effect of imposing burdens, obligations, or disadvantages on such individual or group not imposed upon others, or which withholds or limits access to opportunities, benefit and advantages available to other members of society. Distinctions based on personal characteristics attribute to an individual solely on the basis of association with a group will rarely escape the charge of discrimination, while those based on an individual's merits and capacities will rarely be so classed. (*Andrews v. Law Society of British Columbia*, [1989] 2 W.W.R. at 308)[7]

Discrimination: A Fine Line and a Delicate Balance

For many people within institutional settings, the issue of discrimination is a rather grey area. That is to say they are unsure as to what actually constitutes a discriminatory act. There is, no doubt, a fine line between one's personal preferences and their actually performing acts of discrimination. Needless to say, everyone has certain preferences and biases. Indeed everyone is prejudiced, to a degree. Prejudice comes under many guises and rears itself in many forms. It can be blatant and overt, or it can be systemic and built-in, what the author would call "insidious discrimination".

The author contends that the difference between discrimination and prejudice, be it insidious or otherwise, is when one allows his or her feeling, or preferences to guide them whilst taking institutional decisions. So an individual who exercises her or his personal preferences as a

---

[7]   The Supreme Court of Canada re-affirmed Mr. Justice McIntyre's definition of discrimination in the case of *R. v. Turpin* [1989] 1 S.C.R. 1296, 48 C.c.C. (3d) 8.

guiding force in taking decisions within the capacity of their work-related duties is exercising an act of discrimination.

For example, if someone dislikes people of a certain ethnicity, that is their personal preference. Indeed they have the right to freedom of thought and belief as well as the right to associate with whom they wish (see the section of fundamenatl freedoms). But if those beliefs guide their decision whilst hiring teachers, for example, then their prejudice has been transformed into an act of discrimination. They have crossed the line from holding personal preferences to that of abusing their power within an institutional setting.

Once again there is a fine line between personal prejudice and discrimination, but the line does indeed exist and it requires a delicate balance to set one's prejudice and personal feelings aside to take decisions in a "fair" and "impartial" manner. In order to do this, there is a call for reflective practice. Furthermore, there is a call to examine institutional policies and practices to weed out insidious discrimination, particularly at the classroom level where students may be discriminated against based on gender, race or religion. Such practices are unconstitutional under the *Charter*.

Education and Equality Rights Arguments

Education-related cases brought before the courts often involve claims based on more than one *Charter* argument. That is to say, few equality rights arguments are based on the section 15 provision alone. Equality arguments are usually linked with other guarantees under the *Charter* such as fundamental freedoms (section 2) or principles of fundamental justice (section 7). The cases of *Noyes* and *Weinstein*, discussed in the previous chapter, for example, dealt with legal rights, but also with equality rights under section 15.

In the *Noyes* case, the court found no evidence that he had been discriminated against when the school board suspended him from his teaching duties without pay. In the *Weinstein* case, the argument of discrimination was rejected because *Charter* guarantees do not apply to statutory boards. Furthermore, in *McCloud and Randell*, mentioned in the chapter on fundamental freedoms, the plaintiffs argued that mandatory school enrolment violated their equality rights. The Supreme Court of

Newfoundland ultimately rejected this argument and the parents were convicted of failing to enrol their children in school.

An equality argument was alleged in the case of *Trofimenkoff,* where the Court of Appeal upheld a decision that there was no evidence that the Ministry had failed in its duty to provide special educational provisions for disabled students in his decision to close the R. J. D. Williams Provincial School for the Deaf in Saskatchewan.

Other examples involving equality rights arguments with those pertaining to other provisions under the *Charter* arguments include, *Black v. Metropolitan Separate School Board* (1988) and *Casagrande v. Hinton Roman Catholic District No. 155 et al.* (1987), both of which will be discussed later in the chapter on denominational and separate school rights (under section 29 of the *Charter*). In addition, the case of *Re: Constitutional Questions Act, etc. (Manitoba)* [1990], involving section 23 (minority language educational rights) and section 15 (equality rights) will be discussed in the chapter dealing with minority language educational rights.

Reluctance in Equality Arguments

The reluctance on the part of applicants to utilize section 15 as the focal point of their arguments may be attributed to one of two reasons. Firstly, the staggered date of section 15 coming into effect. Section 15 came into force in 1985 and not 1982, like other provisions. Early rulings were accordingly made under different provisions of the *Charter*. This will be discussed in greater detail later in this chapter. Secondly, and perhaps more importantly, the relative ambiguity of the meaning and intent of equality rights, as they pertain to the educational sector will also be discussed.

It is generally held that an equality argument will enhance another *Charter* argument, as opposed to standing alone on its own merits. This phenomenon may be due to the relative age of the *Charter* and a perceived reluctance on the part of judges to wander too far from the *status quo* in issuing equity rulings. This phenomenon will most likely dissipate as more and more rulings are handed down and education-related case law evolves further. Such reluctance has been duly noted in the area of special education. As time passes courts are becoming more involved in the policy area of special education. This will be discussed later in this chapter.

Equality Rights Case Law

To date, there have been no cases regarding affirmative action. Education-related cases dealing principally with equality, involve issues of: teacher leave of absence;   discrimination based on age;   benefit coverage under workers' compensation;   mandatory retirement;   and, special education.

Teacher Leave of Absence: Democratic and Equality Rights

In *Jonson v. County of Ponoka #3* (1988), the plaintiff was elected as a Member of the Alberta Legislative Assembly (M.L.A.). He applied for a leave of absence from his position, as principal of Ponoka Composite High School, for the duration of his tenure as a member of the provincial legislature. The application was refused.

Jonson appealed the decision on equality grounds under the *Charter*. The application was handed over to a Board of Reference, set up in accordance with the Alberta *School Act*. It is important to note that the Board was deemed to be a court of competent jurisdiction, and therefore it could consider *Charter* issues and grant remedies under section 24(1) of the *Charter*.

The Board ultimately refused to grant Jonson a leave of absence without pay. Jonson claimed that this decision offended his *Charter* rights under section 3 (democratic rights) to stand for public office[8] and section 15(1) (equality rights). Jonson also questioned whether the Board of Reference was a "Court of competent jurisdiction" and hence permitted to consider *Charter* issues and grant *Charter* remedies.

The Court of Queen's Bench ruled that the Board of Reference, created in accordance with the *School Act*, was indeed a "Court of

---

[8]   Section 3 states that "Every citizen of Canada has the right to vote in an election of members of the House of Commons or of a legislative assembly and to be qualified for membership therein".

competent jurisdiction" within the meaning of the *Charter*. The Board could consider *Charter* issues and grant remedies under section 24(1) of the *Charter*. The Court, however, reversed the Board of Reference's decision and ordered that Jonson be reinstated as principal of Ponoka Composite High School and be granted a leave of absence without pay for the duration of his term as M.L.A.

Discrimination Based on Age

A case involving equality before the law occurred in *Smith v. Attorney General of Nova Scotia* (1989). Smith claimed discrimination on the basis of her age. She had applied for a teaching position prior to 1 August 1983 and was placed in a Class 4 qualification. Subsequent changes to the classification scheme occurred after the date in which her qualifications were designated. Smith was upset with the changes because had she applied for teacher classification after these changes, she would have been placed in Class 5, with a higher salary, instead of Class 4.

Upon application, the Province refused to change her classification from Class 4 to that of Class 5. As a result, Smith claimed she was discriminated against because of her age. Had she applied for teaching classification later than she did, she would have been placed in a higher class.

The Supreme Court of Nova Scotia ruled that the different treatment was not related to the plaintiff's age but to the time when she applied for classification. She was therefore not discriminated against within the meaning of section 15 of the *Charter*. Whilst her age may have been a factor, it was not an inseparable link.

Equality and Coverage under Workers' Compensation

In the case of *Romaine v. Workers' Compensation Board* (1988), Margaret Romaine questioned the validity of an Alberta regulation (427/81, section 3(1)(A)) which exempts teachers from being covered under the *Workers' Compensation Act*. Romaine was a substitute teacher who was injured at work. Her application for workers' compensation was refused because under the Act, teachers are exempted from receiving compensation benefits.   Romaine claimed discrimination under section 15(1) of the *Charter*.

The reason the Alberta teachers were exempted from receiving compensation benefits was that the Alberta Teachers' Association and the Trustees' Association had both requested exemption from Workers' Compensation, a stand they both maintained at the time of the court hearing. As a result, the Court ruled that the exemption of the teaching profession from coverage under *The Workers' Compensation Act* of Alberta did not discriminate against Romaine within the meaning of section 15 of the *Charter*. The Court could not see how the purpose and the intent of the Act could discriminate against teachers when they were the ones who had initially requested the exemption.

Equality and the Rights of Unions and Collective Bargaining

The Nova Scotia Government enacted the *Public Sector Compensation Restraint Act* in 1991. This legislation imposed a freeze on the compensation plans of certain public employees for two years. In *Re: Nova Scotia Teachers' Union et al. and the Attorney-General of Nova Scotia; Nova Scotia Government Employees Union, Intervenor* (1993) the unions representing Nova Scotia teachers and Government employees brought an application before the courts to declare the *Compensation Restraint Act* to be in violation of section 2(d), freedom of association, and section 15(1), equality rights, of the *Charter*.

The Nova Scotia Supreme Court held, firstly, that the Act did not violate freedom of association as per section 2(d) because this section did not protect a right to collective bargaining. Secondly, the Act did not violate the equality rights in section 15(1) even though it did result in differential treatment under the law between public sector and private sector employees. In this regard, the Court refused the union's arguments that "employment status" is a personal characteristic or analogous ground necessary to bring it within the ambit of a section 15(1) analysis.

Equality, Mandatory Retirement and Teaching Contracts

In the case of *Ontario English Catholic Teachers' Association v. Essex*

County Roman Catholic Separate School Board (1987), the applicants claimed that mandatory retirement violated their equality rights under section 15(1) of the *Charter*. The School Board terminated a teacher's contract of employment in accordance with the mandatory retirement policy. The Ontario High Court stated that the *Charter* had no application because this issue fell under a contractual agreement between an employer and the employee, and not between an individual and the state.

Although under section 52 of the *Constitution Act 1982*, the courts can strike down laws which violate the *Charter*, in this case neither the mandatory retirement policy nor the resolution to terminate the contract were regarded as law and therefore the *Charter* did not apply.[9]

Equality, Mandatory Retirement and Discrimination Based on Age

In a successfully argued case involving the issue of mandatory retirement, the plaintiff also claimed discrimination based on age. In *Lewis v. Burnaby School District No. 41* (1992), Ms. Lewis worked as a teacher for the Burnaby School District for 27 years. At age 65, the Board required her to retire from teaching in accordance with the then existing section 147 of the British Columbia *School Act*. She challenged the constitutionality of section 147 by arguing that it discriminated against her on the basis of age.

The British Columbia Supreme Court held that her rights under section 15(1) had indeed been violated. Moreover, the violation could not be justified under section 1 of the *Charter*. Between Ms. Lewis' first court appearance and the final judgement, however, the province had repealed section 147 of the Act, and the Board of School Trustees for Burnaby had developed its own policy regarding mandatory retirement.

At the time of the court hearing it was uncertain whether the School Board's new policy on mandatory retirement would be subject to *Charter* review. The Court would not rule on the merits of the new policy because it was outside the scope of the hearing. Thus, for practical reasons, the Court decided to award the teacher damages instead of re-instating her. The Court stated; "reinstatement may be a hollow remedy

---

[9]   Leave to appeal to the Supreme Court of Canada was refused (1988).

for the petitioner if she is immediately forced to retire under the board's present policy" (71 B.C.L.R. (2d), p. 194).

Mandatory Retirement and Teaching Contracts

It should be noted that the difference in the above mentioned cases is quite significant. In the *Essex County* case, on the one hand, the policy was that of a school board and thus one step removed from the arm of Government. It was therefore not considered an action of the state *per se*. Bearing in mind that the purpose of the *Charter* is to protect the individual against wrongs perpetrated by the state, the retirement policy was not a direct action (and indeed too indirect an action) to be considered under the auspices of the state.

In *Lewis*, on the other hand, the mandatory retirement policy was stated directly in the British Columbia *School Act* and thus constituted a direct action of the state. As a result, the state had violated her equality rights and she was thus eligible for compensation. Since the new retirement policy was under the control of the Board of School Trustees for Burnaby, she was likely to lose her case (as in the instance of *Essex County*). The new policy was one step too far removed from the arm of Government to actually constitute an act perpetrated by the state. It was now between an employer and an employee.

Although this may not seem like an important distinction, it is, because it changes the relationship between teachers and their employers. It would seem that the *Charter* does not apply to issues of a contractual nature between teachers and boards of education. They are effectively treated in an employer/employee fashion unless there is direct provincial legislation regulating their relationship.

Right of Spouses to Teach at the Same School

An interesting case which was heard in relation to a provincial human rights code and not the *Charter per se*, but pertinent to this section because it examines issues pertaining to the rights of teachers, involved the issue of whether teaching spouses could teach at the same school. In the case of *Marquardt v. Peace River South School District 59* (1990) the

British Columbia Human Rights Council examined a school policy which effectively prohibited "spousal teachers" from teaching at the same school. The Human Rights Council found such a policy to violate the *Human Rights Act* of British Columbia stating that it should not constitute a *bona fide* requirement for employment.

Equality and Special Education

Arguments alleging discrimination on the basis of mental and physical disability are increasing in many court and tribunal hearings. The educational needs and rights of exceptional children involve issues that are neither easily defined nor resolved. Numerous instances have come forward regarding student identification and placement in special education programmes. The predominant issue in recent court cases involves discrimination based on mental or physical disability as per section 15(1). However, the early cases focused on other arguments under the *Charter* such as freedom of association and life, liberty, and security.

In the case of *Maw* (1983) (discussed in Chapter Four on legal rights), three applicants sought orders to quash decisions by the Etobicoke and Scarborough Boards of Education. These Boards would not hold "hard to serve pupil" hearings for three "exceptional" children until these children were enrolled in the respective Boards of Education. The Court upheld the Boards' position stating that boards of education are only required to hold these hearings for students who are enrolled with the said Board. The children in question were not enrolled as students with the respective Boards.

In the case of *Bales v. Board of School Trustees (Central Okanagan)* (1984) (also addressed in the chapter on legal rights), the parents argued the right under section 7, to have their child attend a regular school and not one for special needs students. The Court dismissed their application. Justice Taylor, of the Supreme Court of British Columbia, ruled that the evidence provided supported the conclusions that segregated schooling did not harm the child and that the School Board had acted appropriately.

It should be noted that the cases of *Maw* and *Bales* went to court before the equality rights provision of the *Charter* came into effect in 1985. Since these cases, several other special education cases have been the centre of much debate concerning discrimination under section 15(1). Cases such as *Elwood* (1986), *Rowett* (1989), *Robichaud* (1989) and *Eaton* (1997) are important whilst examining special education under section 15 of the *Charter*.

Special Education: Segregation and Irreparable Harm

In *Elwood* (1986), the parents were successful in securing an interlocutory injunction to keep their son in an integrated class setting. Luke Elwood was a mentally handicapped boy classified as "trainable mentally handicapped". He attended an integrated pre-school programme for three years and was later placed in a special education class. In 1986, Mr. and Mrs. Elwood enrolled Luke in a regular age-appropriate class at another school. The School Board subsequently decided to have Luke return to the special education class. At this point, however, the Elwoods sought and received an interim injunction to prevent the Board from making Luke return to the special education class. In an interlocutory motion, the Elwoods claimed the Board's decision violated Luke's rights under section 2(d) freedom of association, section 7 life, liberty, and security, and section 15(1) equality rights.

Madam Justice Glube ruled that Luke would "suffer irreparable harm" should the injunction be lifted before going to trial. The Elwoods and the Board of Education reached an agreement shortly before the trial was set to be heard by the Supreme Court of Nova Scotia. Although the *Charter* arguments were not specifically addressed in the agreement, this case illustrates how educational decisions have been shaped by *Charter* arguments.

Courts rarely grant interim injunctions of this nature. Regardless of the overall issue (regarding "irreparable harm" and "a balance of convenience"), courts tend to leave the substantive questions to the trial court and not "grant the remedy in advance". There is little doubt that the interlocutory injunction (the remedy) caused the Board to eventually acquiesce to the Elwoods' demands in reaching their out-of-court settlement.[10]

---

[10]   For further discussion on the *Elwood* case see: Black-Branch, J. L. (1993b) Judicial Intervention, the Balancing of Interests and Administrative Decision-Making:

Special Education Tribunals and Jurisdiction

Rowett (1989) dealt with the placement of a Down's Syndrome child. Joclyn Rowett was identified as "developmentally delayed". It was decided that she should be placed in a self-contained classroom. This meant that Joclyn would have to be bussed to a special school outside her neighbourhood. The parents challenged the school's decision. They contended that the placement contravened their daughter's rights to equal protection, treatment and benefit of the law, guaranteed under section 15(1).

The Special Education Tribunal that first heard the challenge questioned its authority to consider *Charter* arguments but, in any event, they did not see an apparent breach of Joclyn's section 15 rights. The Supreme Court of Ontario ruled that the Special Education Tribunal was "not a court of competent jurisdiction" for the purposes of section 24 of the *Charter*. As a result, the Tribunal had no jurisdiction to consider the Rowetts' *Charter* arguments. The Ontario Court of Appeal later overturned this ruling stating, "it is impossible at this stage to determine the exact bounds of relevancy. The factual and legal issues are inextricably intertwined and can be dealt with more effectively when evidence is adduced at trial".

Special Education and the Jurisdiction of the Courts

In the case of *Robichaud v. Nouveau-Brunswick (La Commission Scolaire Numero 39)* (1989), the parents of Nathalie, a "developmentally handicapped" child, sought a remedy when the Board of Education decided to place Nathalie in a special education class rather than a regular one. At the time, New Brunswick legislation required that exceptional children be "mainstreamed" (integrated) into regular classes, and be given special individualized programmes. Nathalie had not been mainstreamed and her parents argued that this violated her equality rights under the *Charter*.

Using the Canadian Charter of Rights and Freedoms as a Vehicle for Parental Participation in Settling Disputes Regarding Programme, *Canadian Journal of Special Education Vol. 9, No. 1.*

The trial judge agreed that Nathalie's equality rights had been violated. He granted a mandatory injunction, ordering Nathalie to be placed in a regular grade eight class. In addition, he ordered that a committee be formed to assist in her integration into this class, as the provincial guidelines regarding these matters stipulated. Prior to this ruling, the School Board had not yet begun instituting the provincial mandate concerning the "mainstreaming" of exceptional students.

The New Brunswick Court of Appeal, however, reversed this decision. The Court ruled there were "insufficient grounds to grant the injunction". There was not enough evidence that Nathalie would suffer irreparable harm in a special education class, rather than a regular one. Further, the Court stated: "We are of the opinion that the preparation of a plan for exceptional pupils is not a question of law and does not fall within the court's jurisdiction." The Court hence supported the school's decision to have Nathalie placed in a special education class.

Special Education and Catholic Schooling

In the case of *Lanark, Leeds & Grenville Roman Catholic Separate School Board v. Ontario* (1987) (Human Rights Commission), in the end, the court was not willing to intervene in the dealings of the Board. The initial court ruling accepted that the special education students were being denied a "Catholic" education and were discriminated against. This decision was subsequently overturned by a Divisional Court.[11] The Divisional Court stated that the School Board was not compelled to develop the services sought by the parents. The Court was not disposed to making decisions regarding special education. In the Lanark case the Court was reluctant to rule on matters it felt lay outside its jurisdiction, unlike in the *Robichaud* case where the Court did not hesitate to rule on upholding laws that were instituted by the province.

---

11   *Lanark, Leeds & Grenville Roman Catholic Separate School Board v. Ontario* (Human Rights Commission), (sub nom. Hickling v. Lanark, Leeds & Grenville Roman Catholic Separate School Board) (1986), was heard by an Ontario Board of Inquiry. The decision was reversed (1987) by the Ontario Divisional Court which was affirmed (1989) by the Court of Appeal.

Parental Participation, Integration and Special Educational Needs

The recent case of *Eaton v. Brant (County) Board of Education* (1997) saw a reversal of the apparent reluctance on the part of Ontario courts to rule in the area of special education. Initially the Divisional Court dismissed an application for judicial review but later the Ontario Court of Appeal allowed the appeal agreeing with the parents that the Divisional Court had erred in its ruling on the issue on the grounds of discrimination. The Supreme Court of Canada has since restored the Divisional Court ruling.

The case started when Brant (County) Board of Education requested that the Board's Identification, Placement and Review Committee (IPRC) place Emily, a ten-year-old girl with cerebral palsy, into a special class for disabled students. The IPRC agreed with the decision, against the wishes of Emily's parents. The decision was subsequently upheld by the Special Education Appeal Board and later by the Ontario Special Education (English) Tribunal.

Emily's parents then appealed to the Divisional Court for judicial review of the Tribunal's decision on the grounds of discrimination under section 15(1) of the *Charter*. The Divisional Court dismissed the application for review stating its "difficulty in appreciating how the *Canadian Charter of Rights and Freedoms* and the Ontario *Human Rights Code* create a presumption in favour of one pedagogical theory over another" (22 O.R. (3d) 1).

The parents appealed this decision on the grounds that both the Tribunal and the Divisional Court erred in that they applied a legal test that was inherently discriminatory whilst determining Emily's placement. That is to say, "The Tribunal clearly rejected any notion of a presumption in favour of inclusion of disabled children into regular classrooms, or of imposing upon the school board a requirement of demonstrating the superiority of a segregated placement for E[mily] over the educational experience that she was obtaining in an integrated classroom" (22 O.R. (3d) 1). The parents argued that such a presumption and such a burden were indeed mandated under section 15(1) of the *Charter*.

The Court of Appeal agreed with these arguments. Analysing the decision to educate Emily in a special classroom in its social, historical and political context,[12] the Court felt that the decision at hand placed a "burden" or a "disadvantage" on Emily which amounted to discriminatory practice within the meaning of section 15(1). In addition, the Court pointed out that distinctions based on mental and physical ability under section 15 were not to be taken less seriously than those involving sex or race. That is to say, there is no hierarchy of grounds for discrimination. Each category is to be viewed with the same degree of scrutiny as any other.

Further, the Court did not feel that the discretion conferred upon school boards to segregate disabled students, as per section 8(3) of the *Education Act* of Ontario, constituted a reasonable limit prescribed by law within the meaning of section 1 of the limitations clause. The remedy for the situation was to curtail the discretionary powers conferred upon the School Board as per section 8 of the *Education Act*. That is to say, "unless the parents of a disabled child consent to the placement of that child in a segregated environment, the school board must provide a placement that is the least exclusionary from the mainstream and still reasonably capable of meeting the child's special needs" (22 O.R. (3d) 2).

The Supreme Court of Canada has since overturned this ruling, however. It concluded that, "the placement of Emily which was confirmed by the Tribunal did not constitute the imposition of a burden or disadvantage nor did it constitute the withholding of a benefit or advantage from the child".[13] The Court thus found no violation of section 15, stating: "The approach that the Tribunal took is one that is authorized by the general language of s[ection] 8(3) of the [Education] Act." And, that approach "conforms" with section 15(1) of the *Charter*. The Supreme Court of Canada thus moved to restore the Divisional Court's ruling.

Élitist Tendencies in Judicial Rulings: Special Education

There appear to be two prevalent political ideologies in relation to special

---

[12]   In *R. v. Turpin* [1989] the Supreme Court of Canada stated that, "the *indicia* of discrimination must be found in the social, historical and political context surrounding the measure which is alleged to be discriminatory" (22 O.R. (3d) 13).

[13]   Quoted from unpublished documents of the Supreme Court of Canada rulings (File No.: 24668), page 45 of 47.

education. In some instances the school knows what is best and in other instances, integration into mainstream settings is an ever-increasing priority within educational institutions. In some instances the judiciary is reluctant to become involved with the affairs of the school (e.g., *Bales*; *Maw*; *Lanark, Leeds & Grenville*; *Rowett*; and, *Robichaud*). As a result, there is very little examination of the merits of the issues at stake. In these instances the courts favour the *status quo*, that is the School Board, over parental interests.

Other courts, however, are increasingly accepting their role in weighing the merits in such cases. Such a trend began with the *Elwood* ruling whereby an injunction was issued and the merits of the case were to be weighed in court, although in this instance the issue was subsequently settled out-of-court. Although the judge did not rule on the merits of the case *per se*, it was thought that failing to issue an injunction to keep Elwood in the mainstream setting may have resulted in irreparable harm. This provided strong support for parental involvement in issues of placement.

The latest case of *Eaton* initially provided even stronger support for parental participation in the process of special needs placements. In this case, the Ontario Court of Appeal allowed for an appeal based on grounds of discrimination regarding a segregated classroom situation. The approach by the Court of Appeal set the stage for an ever-increasing support of the politically popular notion of mainstreaming and integration over that of segregation.

As the Court of Appeal stated in *Eaton*, in curtailing the discretionary powers of the Board as per the *Education Act*, the Board "must provide a placement that is the least exclusionary from the mainstream". That is, of course, providing the parents of a disabled child actually consent to a placement in a segregated environment.

The Supreme Court of Canada has since removed this requirement, sending a powerful signal to schools and to the community at large that the courts are not prepared to support the notion of integration and mainstreaming over the old adage that "the educator knows what is best for the child". (For discussion on political decisions see *Trofimenkoff* in the section on the School for the Deaf: Closure, and Equality presented in Chapter Four.)[14]

---

14   Some would argue that educators should also be concerned with balancing the best

Conclusion: Practical Applications Regarding Equality

The cases involving issues of equality and discrimination deal with an array of issues ranging from the constitutionality of mandatory retirement to that of discrimination based on age. It seems that courts are analysing these issues within their individual contexts and are not moving towards broader trends. Many of these cases focus on procedural issues and relate to whether the *Charter* actually applies in a given situation.

There is little doubt that issues of equality and special education will continue to move to the forefront of both social and political agendas. Needless to say, these agendas will invariably impinge on the economic realities of education. Moving toward a more equitable and inclusive educational system requires vast financial commitment. The costs for ensuring special educational programmes come at great expense to the tax base. This will force educators and educational planners to re-assess their priorities, particularly in light of the current economic constraints.

It may well be decided that expensive sports teams and other large-expense extra-curricular activities will have to be cut from school budgets[15] in order to allow for special facilities and equipment to enable all children to receive equality of opportunity in education. Equality of education is defined as providing an educational environment which enables a child to develop to her or his fullest potential, academically and talent-wise, regardless of ability or challenges pertaining thereto.

Conversely, public outcry may sway political ideology in the other

---

interests of other members of the class. For example, the most effective way of teaching skills is by direct instruction. If special needs students are disruptive (intentionally or unintentionally), direct instruction becomes impossible. Thus, placing disruptive students in a regular class can be a detriment to other children. There may be far-reaching effects. For example, some parents, believing their child is not getting sufficient attention may transfer their child to another class (such as a French immersion programme which are not typically occupied by extreme special needs students), or indeed to a private school. If several parents take such action, the effect on the remaining class members may be more severe. This issue is vital because it illustrates one of the problems with introducing individual rights into social institutions where a major concern is that of the collective. A delicate balance of the two is necessary.

15   School boards may increasingly turn to the private sector to access funds for extra-curricular activities. An example of this is the recent move by Toronto Board of Education to accept financial endorsement from a major soft drinks company. Whether this will lead to the commercialization of public education remains to be seen.

direction, which may invariably influence courts to reverse current trends and actually restrict the rights of special needs children, in accordance with political pressure.   It seems the courts tend to follow the political *status quo* (see discussion in Chapter 9).

6 Minority Language Educational Rights

Introduction

Prior to the institution of the *Canadian Charter of Rights and Freedoms*, linguistic rights were protected under the *Official Languages Act 1970*. The *Official Languages Act* is a federal statute and hence does not have the same legal strength as the *Charter*. In addition, this federal Act made provisions for essential services and did not make express provisions in relation to educational language rights. Not only does the *Charter* provide for these rights, but it sets the stage for linguistic equity in educational institutions for both francophones and anglophones throughout the country, regardless of provincial language restrictions.

Linguistic Equality

The *Canadian Charter of Rights and Freedoms* clearly stipulates that both English and French are the official languages of Canada, each having equal "status" and to be given equal "privilege". Each of these official languages is to be respected by the three arms of Government, namely the House of Parliament,[1] the Executive and the Courts. Section 16 of the *Charter* states:

> 16(1)   English and French are the official languages of Canada and have equality of status and equal rights and privileges as to their use in all institutions of the Parliament and government of Canada.

---

[1]   The Canadian system of governance operates on what is called a bicameral system. That is, there are two separate chambers within the House of Parliament, a lower chamber to which members are elected (Members of Parliament -- MPs) and an upper chamber (the Senate) to which individuals are appointed (Senators).

A Dual-Language State

Beyond this reaffirmation of a dual-language state, for a bilingual and a bicultural society, is the guarantee of educational language rights for both these groups of citizens.   That is to say, both French and English Canadians are "entitled", under constitutional law, to have their children educated in their first language.   The *Canadian Charter* is unique in its endorsement of educational linguistic rights.   No other country currently makes such a recognition under constitutional law.

Francophone populations are entitled to receive French as a first language education in provinces where English is the majority (official) language (that is all provinces and territories except Québec which is French and New Brunswick which is bilingual[2])[3], just as anglophones are guaranteed English language instruction in the Province of Québec. Section 23 of the *Charter* clearly provides for this, stating that the minority linguistic group has "the right to have their children receive primary and secondary school instruction" in their first language. Specifically, section 23 states:

> 23(1)   Citizens of Canada
> (a)   whose first language learned and still understood is that of the English or French linguistic minority population of the province in which they reside, or[4]
> (b)   who have received their primary school instruction in Canada in English or French and reside in a province where the language in which they received that instruction in the language is English or French linguistic minority

---

[2]   The province of New Brunswick is officially bilingual, guaranteeing education in either official language.

[3]   Shortly after the institution of the *Constitution Act 1982*, the Government of Manitoba requested an amendment to the Constitution recognizing that Province as bilingual.   Federal Parliament did not act on the proposal.   The Supreme Court of Canada has ruled that the Manitoba *Language Act 1890*, which made English the official language is unconstitutional.   The *Manitoba Act 1870* recognizes both English and French as the official languages of the Province.

[4]   According to section 59 of the *Constitution Act 1982*, section 23(1)(a) will only come into effect in the Province of Québec when "authorized by the legislative assembly or government of Québec".   This has not yet been authorized.

population of the province, have the right to have their children receive primary and secondary school instruction in that language in that province.

(2)   Citizens of Canada of whom any child has received or is receiving primary or secondary school instruction in English or French in Canada, have the right to have all their children receive primary and secondary school instruction in the same language.

Language Rights Bestowed on the Parents

An important distinction regarding these rights is that they are bestowed upon the parent and not the child. Hence, in the event of disagreement regarding the realization of these rights, parents make application with the courts on their own behalf and not that of their children.

The Judiciary as a Key Player in Defining Language Rights

As clearly as the *Charter* provides for minority language education, the degree to which these rights may be enforced has sparked controversy and differences of opinion in interpreting the rights bestowed therein. As a result, the judiciary has become an instrumental player in defining minority language educational rights. In fact, the author would contend that, to date, this section of the *Charter* has had the largest influence on a national scale.

Minority Language Educational Rights: An Affirmative Action Clause

Judicial rulings on minority language education issues have expanded the rights of minority language groups throughout Canada. Courts see section 23 as an affirmative action clause, making liberal decisions that seek to remedy past injustices. No doubt, such judicial decisions have profound implications for educational policy throughout Canada. This area of litigation is one of the most fertile areas of *Charter* court action, as is evidenced by the major court actions concerning language rights in all provinces, with the exception of Newfoundland. The very fact that these cases have gone before courts in the first place indicates a change in Canadian tradition.   Before the entrenchment of minority language educational rights, educational linguistic issues were largely decided during political debates, often taking second place to other priorities. Since the institution of the *Charter* this has changed.

Charter case law involving minority language educational rights encompasses a number of concerns.   The issues include: defining legitimate minority language rightholders; specifying numerical values to warrant sufficient numbers of minority language students for instruction, and, separate facilities; determining the degree and scope of management and control of instruction and, consequently, facilities; questioning the right to public funding; allowing for education equivalent to that of the majority language group; scrutinizing existing territorial boundaries for determining numbers of minority language students;   and, assessing denominational considerations pertaining to minority language education.[5]

Defining Minority Language Rightholders

Charter definitions pretaining to those eligible as minority language rightholders have drawn perhaps the least debate.   This is one *Charter* section that clearly defines the benefactors of the provision.   Three distinct groups of Canadian citizens qualify to have their children receive minority language instruction.   These are: (1) Those whose first language learned and still understood is English or French and are of the minority linguistic group;   (2) Those who have received their primary school instruction in Canada in English or French and that language is the minority language in the province in which they currently live; (3) Those who have a child that has received or is receiving primary or secondary school instruction in English or French in Canada.

---

[5]   For further discussion on the minority language educational rights see: Black-Branch, J. L. (1992b) *Minority Language Educational Rights: A Constitutional Right In Canada*.   A paper presented at the VIIIth World Congress of Comparative Education, Prague, Czechoslovakia; and Black-Branch, J. L. (1992c) *Minority Language Rights: A Canadian Example*.   Paper presented at the European Conference on Educational Research, Enschede, The Netherlands.

Eligible Minority Language Rightholders

There were two cases regarding legitimate minority language rightholders under section 23. The first case involved a conflict between the wording of Bill 101 in Québec and section 23 of the *Charter*, while the second case involved an application by three sets of people claiming to be minority language rightholders in British Columbia.

Minority Language Rights for English-Speaking Quebeckers

The case of *Attorney General of Québec v. Québec Association of Protestant School Boards et al.* [1984] involved judicial scrutiny of Québec legislation. Specific provisions regarding access to English language education contained in Bill 101, Ch. VIII of *la Charte de la langue française* (R.S.Q. 1977, v. C - 11) and the regulations thereunder were said to discriminate against some minority language rightholders. These sections specified which children were eligible to receive English language instruction in the Province of Québec. But some of these provisions were inconsistent with section 23 of the *Charter of Rights and Freedoms*.

Specifically, Canadians moving to the Province of Québec after 1977 who had not been educated in the minority language (English) in the Province of Québec were not eligible to have their children receive English language instruction in that province. According to the *Charter of Rights and Freedoms*, however, Canadians who were educated in the English language elsewhere in Canada are eligible to have their children educated with English as the language of instruction, regardless of the province of origin.

The Supreme Court of Canada ruled that the provisions under Ch. VIII of *la Charte de la langue française,* specifically, section 72 and section 73, were inconsistent with the provisions as listed in section 23 of the *Charter of Rights and Freedoms*. The Court had no problem in reaching this decision. The Court struggled, however, with the issue of trying to balance the arguments for limiting such rights, under the limitations clause in the *Charter*. In the end, the Court did not rule whether limiting these English minority language rights was demonstrably justified under section 1 of the *Charter*.

In essence, not answering whether these rights should be limited under section 1 was, in fact, a decision which upheld English minority language rights. The provisions (section 72 and section 73) limiting such instruction were judged to be "of no force or effect" under section 52 of the *Charter*. This important case thus expanded the educational rights of anglophone Canadians originating from other provinces, but residing in Québec.

Minority Language Rights and French Immersion

A second case relating to the question of eligibility to receive minority language instruction as rightholders was *Whittington et al. v. Board of School Trustees of School District No. 63 (Saanich)* (1987). The Supreme Court of British Columbia heard this case in which a respondent school board had terminated an early French immersion (E.F.I.) programme at the kindergarten level. Parents belonging to three distinct categories petitioned to have the Board reinstate the E.F.I. program.

The first category of petitioners consisted of English-speaking Canadians who, at the time, had children enrolled in the E.F.I. programme and one child commencing kindergarten that September. They argued the right to have all their children taught in French as stated in section 23(2) of the *Charter*. The second category was a parent whose child had attended kindergarten the previous year and who was going to repeat kindergarten. This parent argued that her son had "lost his right" to the E.F.I. programme. The third category was a parent whose first language learned and still understood was French. She argued the right, as a section 23 rightholder under 23(1)(a), to have her child enrol in the E.F.I. programme at the kindergarten level.

Mr. Justice Proudfoot, identifying section 23(2) as central to the issue, asked the following questions:

Does section 23(2) provide citizens of Canada who have a child enrolled in a French immersion programme with a constitutional right to have all their children educated in a French immersion programme? Does an anglophone majority population have the constitutional right to receive their education in the minority language of the province? Does section 23(2) of the *Charter* provide the citizens of Canada, residents of British Columbia a majority English linguistic group, with the right to have their children educated in a French immersion programme? (16 B.C. L.R. (2d) pp. 258-259)

He decided that section 23 refers to rights of the English or French linguistic minority in each province, to have their children receive education in the minority language. The first two categories of parents were of the majority linguistic group in British Columbia (English). As a result, these parents were not legitimate claimants under section 23. Specifically, Proudfoot J stated that section 23(2) provides the right to obtain instruction in French as the primary (first) language, but this right therefore can only be conferred on a citizen who has received instruction in that language. The children involved were receiving instruction in French immersion which, in essence, is a French as a second language programme within an English majority school system. These children were not receiving French as a first language education, which is what is guaranteed under section 23. Therefore "to accept the petitioners' argument that the words 'instruction in French' in 23(3) convey a right to the English linguistic majority in British Columbia to be educated in the French language, would indeed be to overshoot the actual purpose [of section 23 of the *Charter*]" (16 B.C. L.R. (2d) p. 266).

The parent in the third category was eligible to have her child receive French minority language instruction. Once again, however, the E.F.I. programme was not considered a French as a first language programme of instruction. It is a French immersion programme for the English majority. In the words of Proudfoot J.: "This is an optional programme offered by local school districts. French is taught as a second language in that programme, recognizing English as the primary or first language" (16 B.C. L.R. (2d) p. 266). As a result, the minority language rightholder was not entitled under section 23 to have her child enrol in an immersion class. French instruction falls under the "Cadre de Français" programme which is offered throughout the province, where numbers warrant.

The Status of Minority Language Eligibility

These two cases (*Québec Association of Protestant School Boards* and *Whittington*) dealt with the central issue of who is eligible as minority rightholders.   The first case dealt with conflicting intents between the *Charter* and Québec legislation under Bill 101.   The Court had no problem in agreeing, firstly, with the inconsistency in wording between the two provisions and, secondly, that the *Charter* wording overrides the provincial statutes.   The Court did have trouble, however, in deciding whether the limitation clause of section 1 of the *Charter* should override section 23 and uphold the provincial legislation.   That is, whether limiting such language rights would be demonstrably justified within a free and democratic society.

The second case focused on specific individuals with special circumstances.   In the ruling it was clearly stated that French immersion programmes offer French as a second language to the majority English group.   Majority populations of this nature do not fall under the auspices of section 23.   Further, whilst legitimate minority language rightholders are "entitled" to having their children receive instruction in their first language, they are not "entitled" to programmes offered to the majority group.

Restrictions, Discretionary Power and the Numbers Warrant Test

Reference Re: Education Act of Ontario and Minority Language Education Rights (1984) was heard by the Ontario Court of Appeal. This judgement, concerning the constitutionality of certain sections of the Ontario *Education Act* and proposed amendments to the Act, set precedent on minority language issues that other courts throughout Canada have since followed.

In the *Reference*, section 258 and section 261 of the Ontario *Education Act* were judged to be inconsistent with the *Canadian Charter of Rights and Freedoms* in at least four ways. Specifically, the sections of the *Education Act* were ruled as placing improper restrictions on the beneficiaries of section 23 *Charter* rights. Under these sections only those French-speaking pupils wishing to be taught in French were to be included in determining the actual number of students eligible for minority language instruction. As a result, the numbers of eligible students would be lower than the numbers envisioned by the section 23 test.

In addition, the provisions of the *Education Act* left it to the discretion of the school board to determine whether the number of pupils was sufficient to provide elementary schooling. The provisions of the Act also conferred wide discretionary powers on school boards regarding the establishment of French language secondary schools. The Court ruled the "numbers warrant" test provided in the Act (which stated that boards needed to provide French language instruction only where it was practicable to assemble classes of twenty-five for primary schools and twenty for secondary schools) was too rigid and inconsistent with the intent of section 23.

The Court also ruled that section 23 rights should transcend the geographical boundaries of school boards; the existing territorial limitation of school boards placed restrictions on language rights. Furthermore, the Court decided that the members of the French linguistic minority in Ontario were not only entitled to have their children receive instruction in the French language but also, they had the right to manage and control their own French language classes of instruction and French language educational facilities. Similar court decisions reverberated across Canada after the *Reference* decision.

Instruction, Facilities and Equality

The case of *Marchand v. Simcoe County Board of Education et al.* (1986) provided the impetus for further changes in the Province of Ontario, in general, and in the County of Simcoe in particular. Jacques Marchand (a minority language rightholder) claimed that Simcoe County Board of Education fell short of its constitutional duties, thus violating minority language educational provisions under the *Charter*.

L'École Secondaire Le Caron, a French language secondary school in Penetanguishene was established by the Simcoe Board of Education and was the only school in the Board where secondary education was offered with French as the language of instruction. Marchand sought several distinct court declarations concerning the Simcoe County Board of Education and the Province of Ontario, in regard to French-language education at Le Caron.

Declarations Sought Against: Simcoe County Board of Education and The Province of Ontario

(1)   The number of children whose parents have the right to have their children receive secondary school instruction in the French language in French language educational facilities in or near the Town of Penetanguishene is sufficient to warrant the provision of such instruction and facilities out of public funds;

(2)   Marchand and other minority language rightholders have the right to have their children receive secondary school instruction in the French language in French language educational facilities which are equivalent to the instruction and facilities provided by the Board in English language secondary school facilities in the County of Simcoe, and that this right has been denied or infringed.

Declarations Sought Against: The Province of Ontario

(1)   The Province of Ontario is under a duty to ensure that the French language secondary school instruction and educational facilities provided to the children of Marchand and other minority language rightholders are equivalent to English language secondary school instruction and educational facilities provided within the County of Simcoe, and that such duty includes the provision of adequate funding for such purposes.

Declarations Sought Against: Simcoe County Board of Education

(1)   An order requiring the board to provide facilities and funding necessary to achieve at L'École Secondaire Le Caron the provision of instruction and facilities equivalent to those provided to English language secondary schools within the board.

(2)   An order requiring the board to establish at L'École Secondaire Le Caron facilities for industrial arts and shop programmes equivalent to those provided to English language secondary schools within the board. (55 Ontario Reports, p. 649)

Mr. Justice Sirois, of the High Court of Justice, stated that after the 1984 *Reference* case, the case involving Marchand should never have reached the Court. It should have been "resolved amongst the parties" (55 O.R. (2d) p. 650). With this in mind, the High Court ruled that Simcoe County Board of Education was to declare that there were sufficient numbers of children to warrant French language secondary school instruction. Further, they would be eligible for educational facilities in or near the Town of Penetanguishene and their children would receive these educational provisions.

In fact, Sirois J. stated it was the "duty" of Her Majesty the Queen in right of Ontario to ensure French language secondary schooling and facilities within the County of Simcoe. These programmes and facilities were to be provided out of public funds and were to be equivalent to that of the English language majority. The judge went one step further, actually naming specific programmes and facilities to be offered and housed at l'École Secondaire Le Caron. In particular, the Board was to provide a shop programme with full industrial arts facilities equivalent to those provided in English language secondary schools.[6]

Management and Control and Territorial Limitations

The 1984 Ontario *Reference* case was one of the strong forces guiding the judiciary in the *Marchand* case and as well in the *Fransaskoises* (1988) case. The case of *Commission des Écoles Fransaskoises Inc. et al. v. Government of Saskatchewan* [1988] concerned issues of management and

---

6   For further discussion on the *Marchand* case see: Black-Branch, J. L. (1992d) *Recognising Minority Language Educational Rights In A Reemergent Canada: Marchand v. Simcoe County Board of Education.* Paper presented for the Canadian Society for the Study of Education, Charlottetown, P.E.I., Canada.

control, territorial limitations and preconditions regarding minority language instruction. At the time of this case, any board of education in the Province of Saskatchewan that offered programmes with French as a first language of instruction could request designation as a French language school. The regulations pertaining thereto required a guaranteed minimum enrolment of fifteen students for a period of at least three consecutive years. Parents of the minority language group had no rights to management or control over the designated programme. In addition, the plaintiffs argued there was a significant difference between the French and the English schools.

The Saskatchewan Court of Queen's Bench concluded that section 180 of the Saskatchewan *Education Act,* and section 40(2)(b) and (c) of the regulations made thereunder, were "of no force or effect" as they were inconsistent with section 23 of the *Charter.* Section 180 failed to recognize section 23(3)(b) rights to minority management and control of instruction, while section 40(2)(b) placed territorial limitations on the jurisdictions of boards of education thus failing to recognize section 23 rights. Section 40(4)(c) established preconditions to school instruction in French where sufficient numbers of eligible children may have warranted such instruction.

In the case of *Commission des Écoles Fransaskoises et al. v. the Government of Saskatchewan* (1991) the appellants sought an order from the Saskatchewan Court of Appeal to enact minority language legislation. Despite the fact that the Court found that the Saskatchewan legislation was deficient, it ruled that a new trial with evidence was necessary before it could make such an order. The application was thus dismissed. The Court felt that these issues were adequately addressed by the Supreme Court of Canada in *Mahé* (to be discussed in greater detail later in this chapter).[7]

Parental Participation in Programme Development and Delivery

In the case of *Reference Re Minority Language Educational Rights (P.E.I.)* (1988) the Prince Edward Island Court of Appeal examined five

---

7   In *Commission des Écoles Fransaskoises*, leave to appeal to the Supreme Court of Canada was refused on 15 August 1991.

major questions concerning the constitutionality of the *School Act*.   A group of parents in the Summerside area requested the establishment of a grade one French language class.   The Board ruled against such a move stating there were too few students to do so.   The Minister of Education refused to intervene in the dispute.   The parents challenged the School Board's decision in court.

The Court examined who minority language rightholders were under section 23;   territorial limits;   the request for minority language instruction;   section 50(3) (of the P.E.I. *School Act*), allowing for the provision of French language instruction but not the provision of "educational facilities";   and, issues regarding the numbers required to warrant minority language instruction.

The Court recognized that section 23 rights were a "political compromise".   The Court first acknowledged the applicants as minority rightholders within the meaning of section 23 of the *Charter*.   It then decided that section 5.32(1) of the *School Act*, which set geographical limitations on school board boundaries, was inconsistent with the *Charter*. In addition, the Court ruled that either the legislature or the Lieutenant Governor-in-Council could set specific numbers, in reference to the numbers warrant test of the *Charter*, in order to ensure consistency and fairness in all regions of the province.   Specifically, the Court stated that there was no evidence to suggest that the number provision of "twenty-five students [distributed] within three consecutive grade levels" was "unfair or unreasonable".

Further, the Court decided that in situations in which the numbers of students were insufficient to warrant minority language instruction, the Board could arrange other alternatives, such as transporting students to other areas, as outlined in the *School Act*.   Finally, the Court ruled that, for the parents, the "right to participate in French language program development and delivery is implicit in section 23".   The legislature was left to enact provisions regarding section 23 rightholders' participation in French language programme development and delivery.   But since in this case, the Prince Edward Island Legislature had not done so, the *School Act* was in violation of section 23.

Equality Rights for Acadians

In the case of *Lavoie et al. v. Attorney-General of Nova Scotia* (1989), as in the *Marchand* case, the Court ruled there were sufficient numbers of students to warrant minority language education but, unlike the *Marchand* case, there were not sufficient numbers to warrant minority language facilities. Further, the plaintiffs argued that Acadian and anglophone children were treated differently and this amounted to unconstitutional practice under section 23.

The Nova Scotia Supreme Court, Appeal Division, ruled that the number of children of section 23 rightholders, in the Cape Breton School Board, was sufficient to warrant minority language instruction to be paid for out of public funds. Under section 23 of the *Charter*, these children were entitled to primary and secondary school instruction in the language of the French linguistic minority. The Court also decided, however, that the numbers of children in the Cape Breton School Board were not sufficient to warrant the provisions of separate minority language educational facilities pursuant to section 23(3)(b) of the *Charter*. In addition, the appellants did not bear the burden of proving that the costs of providing minority language education would be reasonable. The Court also ruled that the *Education Act* of Nova Scotia does not contravene section 23 of the *Charter*. The Court saw no denial of equality rights for Acadian children.

Establishing French Language Instructional Units in Ontario

In the case of *Piette v. Sault Ste. Marie Board of Education* (1989), a High Court of Ontario judge granted an interlocutory injunction, requiring the School Board to establish and maintain one or more French language instructional units for the minority language students, pending a trial. The plaintiffs were French minority language rightholders; their children were originally receiving French as a first language education from the Separate School Board in Sault Ste. Marie. These parents claimed that the Separate School Board had somewhat liberal admission policies that permitted many non-francophone students into the French as a first language programme. As a result, the parents were concerned about the quality of education their children were receiving.

These parents (of some fifty children) inadvertently re-directed their tax money, from the Separate Board, to that of the Public School Board and requested the Public Board to establish French language instructional units. The request was defeated at a School Board meeting. The parents then sought a court order requiring the Board to establish the French language instructional units, as required by the *Education Act*. The Ontario High Court granted the injunction. The Court stated: "The rights of the ratepayer are infringed if his or her selected school board fails to provide the minority language instruction guaranteed by the *Canadian Charter of Rights and Freedoms* and reinforced in the Province of Ontario by the *Education Act*."

Language Rights are Political Rights

The case of *Société des Acadiens du Nouveau-Brunswick Inc. et al. v. Association of Parents for Fairness in Education, Grand Falls District 50 Branch* [1986] focused on language rights. La Société des Acadiens sued for an injunction which would restrain an English school board from allowing francophone students to register in its French immersion programmes. In addition, they sought an injunction to prevent further registration into the immersion programmes. In other words, the francophone School Board in the area sought an order to stop the anglophone board from accepting francophone students. The Court of Queen's Bench granted the declaration but refused to issue an injunction. The anglophone School Board accepted the decision and did not appeal the decision. But the association of parents applied for both leave to appeal the decision and an extension of the time for appeal.

The application was originally heard by one judge but the appellants insisted that the request be heard by a bilingual judge. The bilingual judge later handed the matter over to a panel of judges. At the Supreme Court of Canada, the arguments dealt with the right to use English and French in New Brunswick courts. In addition, the appellants appealed to the Supreme Court on the grounds that the New Brunswick Court of Appeal did not have the jurisdiction to grant leave to appeal because the respondents were not parties in the original action (the School Board was) and, they were also applying outside the time limit for making an appeal. Regardless of these facts, the Court decided to hear the case.

In addressing the use of English or French in New Brunswick courts, the Supreme Court distinguished between "legal" and "language" rights. It stated that, "Legal rights are said to be seminal because they are rooted in principle" and in this particular instance language rights are founded upon political compromise. As a result the Court stated that they should "pause before they decide to act as instruments of change with respect to language rights".

The Supreme Court ruled that subsection 19(2) of the *Charter* entitles a party pleading in a court in New Brunswick to be heard in either official language. The member or members of the court should be capable of understanding the proceedings, the evidence and the arguments, written and oral, regardless of the official language used by the parties. Whilst this case turned into an examination of language rights, and not educational rights *per se*, it initially involved education and remains an important case regarding language rights.

Minority Language Rights and Equality

Judicial scrutiny of provincial legislation is a common theme in these cases. In *Attorney General of Québec v. Québec Association of Protestant School Boards et al.* (1984) the Court reviewed the legislation and concluded that certain provisions were "of no force or effect" as they were inconsistent with *Charter* guarantees under section 23. Similarly, in the ruling in *Commission des Écoles Fransaskoises Inc. et al. v. Government of Saskatchewan* sections of the Saskatchewan *Education Act* were struck down for failing to recognize certain minority rights, such as the right to management and control.

In the case of *Re: Constitutional Questions Act, etc. (Manitoba)* [1990], the Manitoba Court of Appeal also scrutinized provincial legislation; this examination involved the issue of sufficient numbers to warrant minority language education. The Court examined the combined effect of section 79(3), (4) and (7) of the Manitoba *Public Schools Act*. It was decided that the combined effect of these sections contravened the numbers test established by section 23. In addition, the Court ruled that the province cannot legislate a specific number to warrant minority language education, nor can the province delegate this responsibility to school boards or other bodies.

In this case the Court ruled that "educational facilities", as outlined in section 23(3)(b), mean a distinct physical setting. However, such facilities are not necessarily housed in a separate building. The Court ruled that section 23 and section 15 (equality rights), when combined, do not necessarily grant the right of management or control with the right to instruction and facilities. Five weeks after this ruling came the monumental Supreme Court decision in *Mahé*.

Educational Management and Governance

The case of *Mahé et al. v. R. in Right of Alberta et al.* (1990) addressed many of the on-going concerns and issues regarding minority language educational rights throughout Canada. On 15 March 1990, the Supreme Court of Canada rendered its decision.[8] This was the first case in which the judiciary examined, in any great detail, rights pertaining to educational management and governance under section 23 of the *Charter of Rights and Freedoms*.

Mahé involved a group of section 23 rightholders who were dissatisfied with the provisions for French language education in the Edmonton, Alberta area. Approximately 3,750 students (between the ages of five and nineteen years), of some 116,788 in the Edmonton area, were children of section 23 rightholders. At the time of the Supreme Court hearing, the Edmonton Roman Catholic Separate School Board was operating a French school for francophones. However, section 23 rightholders argued that they had no measure of "management or control" over the school, because in the existing system, the Edmonton Roman Catholic Separate School Board governed and administered the French language school. The rightholders contended that section 23 entitled francophones in the community to a completely autonomous francophone School Board.

They stated francophones should have complete administrative and governing powers within their jurisdiction. They argued these powers should include separate facilities, staffing, control over the school

---

8   In the case of *Mahé* the Court followed the French version of the *Charter* over that of the English one stating: "Since the French version of s. 23(3)(b) is clearer, it should be adopted by the court" (p. 258).

curriculum, and the election of French language trustees. Such "power and control" should be paid for out of public funds and offer educational facilities and services equivalent to those provided to English speaking students in the province.

The Supreme Court analysed nine issues pertinent to this case, including: *inter alia*, the purpose of section 23 of the *Charter of Rights and Freedoms*;   the meaning and the context of section 23(3)(b); management and control; denominational schools' rights; the "numbers warrant" provision; and, the situation in Edmonton. The Court identified and answered the following Constitutional questions in the *Mahé* case:

> Question 1. Have the rights of the linguistic minority population in metropolitan Edmonton to minority language educational facilities pursuant to section 23(3)(b) of the *Charter* been infringed or denied?

> Answer: Yes.

> Question 2. Does the right to minority language instruction and educational facilities pursuant to section 23(3)(a) and section 23(3)(b) of the *Charter* include management and control by the minority of:
> (a) the instruction?
> (b) the educational facilities?
> If so, what is the nature and extent of such management and control?

> Answer: In metropolitan Edmonton, section 23 grants management and control by the minority in respect of instruction and facilities [in terms set out in the guidelines for management and control to follow].

> Question 3. (a) Are the School Act, R.S.A. 1980, c. S-3, and the regulations passed thereunder inconsistent with or in contravention of section 23 of the *Charter*?

Answer: No, with the exception of Reg. 490/82 which *prima facie* infringes section 23.

(b) If so, is such inconsistency or contravention justified under section 1 of the *Charter*?

Answer: The respondent has not shown that Reg. 490/82 is justifiable under section 1 of the *Charter*.

Question 4.   Are the rights guaranteed by section 23 of the *Charter* affected by the provisions of section 93 of the *Constitution Act, 1867*, section 29 of the *Charter* and section 17 of the *Alberta Act*? If so, how?

Answer: No. (72 Alta. L.R. (2d) p. 299, 300)

These constitutional issues moved the Court to the following decision.

The numbers of minority language students in Edmonton warrant as a minimum the provision of section 23 rights by way of minority language representation on school boards administering minority language schools . . . . The province must enact legislation (and regulations, if necessary) that are in all respects consistent with the provisions of section 23 of the *Charter*. (72 Alta. L.R. (2d) p. 294)

Guidelines for Management and Control

The Supreme Court then went one step further and issued guidelines for the management and control of minority language education.

In order to comply with section 23 of the *Charter*, minority language parents in Edmonton should be granted management and control over minority language instruction and facilities in Edmonton in accordance with the following principles:

(1)   The representation of the linguistic minority on local boards or other public authorities which administer minority language instruction or facilities should be guaranteed;

(2)   The number of minority language representatives on the board should be, at a minimum, proportional to the number of minority language students in the school district, i.e., the number of minority language students for whom the board is responsible;

(3)   The minority language representatives should have exclusive authority to make decisions relating to the minority language instruction and facilities, including:

(a)   expenditures of funds provided for such instruction and facilities;

(b)   appointment and direction of those responsible for the administration of such instruction and facilities;

(c)   establishment of program of instruction;

(d)   recruitment and assignment of teachers and other personnel; and

(e)   making of agreements for education and services for minority language pupils. (72 Alta. L.R. (2d) p. 257 -299)

The pith and substance of these guidelines invariably apply to other jurisdictions throughout Canada.

The Sliding Scale Approach to Minority Language Education

In *Mahé*, the Court offered the above guidelines for management and control in accordance with what it called a "sliding scale" approach to interpreting section 23. "The idea of a sliding scale is simply that s[ection] 23 guarantees whatever type and level of rights and services is appropriate in order to provide minority language instruction for the particular number of students involved" (72 Alta. L.R. (2d) p. 276). In other words, all minority language students are guaranteed instruction. The type of arrangements for this instruction, including whether minority language classes will be housed in school facilities separate from the majority language group, and whether they will attend school in a different school board, which would be governed by minority language school trustees, would depend on the number of minority language children. As the number of students increases, so too do the requirements for separate educational facilities and arrangements for management and control by the minority group.

Although these guidelines were offered as a general guide in the *Mahé* case, they are also intended for other educational jurisdictions throughout Canada. In reference to these guidelines, the Court stated that the minority language and majority language educational systems "need not be identical". However, "funds allocated for the minority language schools must be at least equivalent on a per student basis to the funds allocated to the majority schools" (72 Alta. L.R. (2d) p. 285).

In addition, the Court encouraged that additional funding be allocated to these boards, particularly in the initial stages of the minority language school set-up. That is to say, the above mandate from the Court represents the minimum requirement for management and control of education. Provincial and local authorities are at liberty to offer more autonomy than the minimum requirement. This judicial interpretation of section 23 allows for a wide degree of flexibility in establishing "a variety of different forms of institutional structures which will satisfy the above guidelines" (72 Alta. L.R. (2d) p. 286).

Schools As Linguistic Cultural Centres

A recent case in Manitoba, involving the right to manage and control French language instruction and facilities, was also decided by the Supreme Court in *Reference Re: Public Schools Act (Manitoba)* (1993). In this case the Court reassessed the issue of management and control as per its *Mahé* ruling. The Court ruled that the *Charter* (in accordance with sections 23 and 15) does indeed grant French minority language rightholders the right to manage and control instruction and facilities, finding provisions of the *Public Schools Act* of Manitoba deficient.

The Court examined the application of the sliding scale approach as it pertained to the management and control of language instruction and facilities within the Manitoba context. Reversing the Manitoba Court of Appeal ruling, the Supreme Court reaffirmed their 1990 stand in *Mahé*. The court went one step beyond *Mahé*, however, stating that, "some distinctiveness in the physical setting" of the school should be allowed in order to enhance the school as a "cultural centre".

Denominational Schools and Minority Language Educational Rights

The discussion to this point has focused largely on issues of instruction, facilities, and management and control regarding minority language education. Other issues, however, some of which relate to denominational schools and minority language educational rights, have also emerged. In the case of *Reference Re: Education Act of Ontario and Minority Language Educational Rights* (1984), addressed earlier in this chapter, the Court stated that minority language educational rights apply with equal force and effect to minority language instruction and educational facilities provided within both public and denominational education under Parts IV and V of the Ontario *Education Act*. Further, it is within the legislative authority of the Legislative Assembly of Ontario to amend the *Education Act*, as contemplated in the White Paper of 23 March 1983. This legislation provides for the election of minority language trustees to Roman Catholic separate school boards and their right to exercise certain exclusive responsibilities within these school boards.

In the case of *Griffin v. Commission Scolaire Regionale Blainville Deux-Montagnes et al.* (1989), the Québec Superior Court, District of Terrebonne, Québec decided that the children of English-speaking Roman Catholic parents, as a minority group, are entitled to receive English language secondary school instruction in separate educational facilities. The rights to minority language educational facilities enshrined in section 23(3)(b) "make no express reference to religious or denominational characteristics of the facilities". In effect, section 23 rightholders were not entitled to Roman Catholic minority language instruction in separate facilities. Similarly, in *Mahé* the Supreme Court of Canada stated that rights under section 23 are not affected by these provisions (i.e., section 93 of the *Constitution Act 1867*).

Tuition Fees, Dual-Track Systems and Judicial Review

St. Isidore School District in Alberta opened a regional homogenous French language school, École Heritage, in 1988. Some students from another district, Falher Consolidated School District, decided to attend École Heritage. The students' parents requested that Falher District pay tuition fees to St. Isidore in order to fund their children's education. Falher District refused to make the payments claiming that its dual-track school system met the criteria set out in section 23 and that the Alberta *School Act* gave it discretion to refuse to make the payments. In this case, *Goudreau v. Falher Consolidated School District No.* (1993), the intervenors argued that section 23 of the *Charter* entitled them to send their children to École Heritage.

The provincial Minister of Education directed Fahler District to make the payments. Fahler applied for judicial review to set the Minister's decision aside. During the proceedings, four interested groups applied to be added as parties or intervenors: (1) Four parents from Falher whose children attended École Heritage (parents); (2) A regional body of parents from St. Isidore and Fahler (CREF); (3) The Alberta Federation of Francophone parents (AFF); and, (4) The French-Canadian Association of Alberta (FCAA).

The Alberta Court of Appeal held that the parents and CREF were to be named as defendant parties. Since the Minister of Education's ruling on the interpretation of section 23 could affect the financial interests and substantive *Charter* rights of both parents and CREF, they were appropriate parties to advance their positions before the courts. In addition, the four groups had been involved in extended litigation with the government over section 23 and Fahler's M.L.A. (a member of the Minister's political party) supported Fahler's position.

As for the two provincial bodies (AFF and FCAA), the Court felt that they did not have the same direct interest in the litigation as the parents and CREF. They did, however, have special expertise about the issues facing the Court and were thus added as intervenors. Given the complexity and constitutional nature of the proceedings, the Court decided that a full trial was more appropriate to the resolution of issues rather than simply putting the issue to judicial review.

School Transportation Fee Policy for French Language Instruction

In the case of *Bachmann v. St. James-Assiniboia School Division 2* (1984), the Manitoba Court of Appeal examined a school policy requiring that parents wishing to have their children attend French language instruction may be required to pay part of the transport costs. The Court decided that such a policy discriminated against these parents, particularly in light of the fact that the parents of those attending English language instruction would not have to pay the costs. The Court ruled that such a policy would be invalid.

A Manitoba Court, in *Chaddock v. Mystery Lake School District 2355* [1986], ruled that parents choosing to send their children to French language schools may be asked to pay part of the cost of transportation if they reside more than one mile away from the school but they live within one mile of an English language school.[9]

Minority Language Rights and Special Education

Many people question whether minority language rightholders have the right to have their special needs children educated in their first language. Although it is not expressly stated in section 23, minority language parents have an implied right to have their children educated in their first language, regardless of their educational needs. The nature and scope of the particular services offered will inevitably vary from one province to the next, and even within provincial jurisdictions.[10]

---

[9]   In *Chaddock*, leave to appeal to the Supreme Court of Canada was refused [1987].

[10]   In fact, under section 15 of the *Charter*, all students are guaranteed equality of educational opportunity, regardless of whether they are from the minority or the majority linguistic group.

Minority Language Rights and Home Schooling

Minority language rightholders can request to home instruct their children in their first language. Applications to do so would be filed in accordance with guidelines established by individual provinces. The fact that the applicant is a minority language parent should neither bias nor advantage the application. All applicants, be they of the minority or the majority linguistic group, should be treated in the same manner.

Élitist Tendencies in Judicial Rulings: Minority Language Education

Judicial rulings in the area of minority language educational rights provides the most consistent support for the argument that courts tend to support the political *status quo*. There is little doubt that contemporary political ideology supports the policy of a bi-lingual Canada, the cornerstone of which is based on a dual-language state whereby citizens can send their children to either French or English schools, regardless of the numbers of students in a given geographical area. As evidenced from the discussion throughout this chapter, the courts have wholeheartedly embraced such a notion, regardless of the economic costs to individual jurisdictions or the feelings of the local public (i.e., in the case of *Marchand* where there was much controversy over the issue).

In delivering its judgement in a case in *Société des Acadien du Nouveau Brunswick*, the Supreme Court of Canada distinguished between "legal" and "language" rights. It stated that legal rights are rooted in principle, whilst language rights are founded upon political compromise. Given that, whilst interpreting the minority language educational rights section in the above mentioned court challenges, the judiciary has generally relied on sociological data to determine the "political" intent of section 23. Before offering rulings regarding minority language educational issues, courts typically study documents and political reports to determine what the politicians actually intended when entrenching the section 23 provision under constitutional law.

In the *Mahé* case, for example, the Supreme Court of Canada studied *The Royal Commission on Bilingualism and Biculturalism (Book II)* in trying to reach [in their words] "the purpose" of section 23 of the *Charter*. Similarly, in the *Marchand* case, the Ontario High Court of

Justice examined everything from statements concerning bilingualism, emanating from the 1978 Premiers' Conference in Montréal, to the federal Government paper, *A Time For Action*. In addition, the Court specifically examined the aim of section 23 according to a submission to the Special Joint Committee on the Constitution by the Minister of Justice at the time, Jean Chrétien, who described the purpose of entrenching section 23 in the *Charter*. Court rulings have thus made express reference to the political intent of section 23.

The courts have invariably perceived the political intent behind section 23 as the will to make Canada a dual-language (English and French) state in which minority educational instruction and governance are guaranteed to members of both official language groups. Mr. Justice Sirois upheld this intent in the *Marchand* case, quoting the Federal Government paper, *A Time For Action* which read: "the Federation [of Canada] must guarantee the linguistic equality of its two major communities, the English-speaking and the French-speaking" (55 O.R. (2d) p. 657).

Moreover, the intent of section 23 was to serve as [in the words of the Supreme Court of Canada in *Mahé*] "a remedial provision" to "remedy past injustices regarding minority language educational rights and ensure that they are not repeated in the future" (72 Alta. L.R. (2d) p. 281). This political intent was articulated in no uncertain terms by Jean Chrétien's statement as then Minister of Justice. He stated: "We are seeking also to protect, once and for all, the education rights of francophones outside of Québec. . . . The aim of this initiative is to provide francophones outside of Québec with approximately the same rights as the anglophones in Québec enjoy, or once enjoyed" (cited in 55 O.R. (2d) p. 657). Specifically, experts agree that courts typically regard section 23 as a remedial clause, making liberal decisions that seek to remedy past injustices (Black-Branch, 1993a). To that effect, the Supreme Court of Canada has quite clearly stated that funding must be (at least) equal on a per pupil basis and has actively encouraged provincial governments to provide extra support in the initial stages to ensure equality of facilities between linguist systems.

Minority Language Education: Conclusion

There has been an onslaught of litigation pertaining to minority language educational rights. The courts are consistently ruling in favour of the minority group, particularly for francophones outside Québec. It would appear that the judiciary is upholding the political ideology of their political confrères (at a federal level). As illustrated in cases such as *Marchand*, *Mahé* and *Manitoba*, to name but a few, the courts galvanize into reality the dominant federal political ideology of a strong bilingual state which supports the framework of a compound language situation whereby one can attend French or English schools, regardless of geography (location) or demography (numbers).

It should be noted that the Supreme Court of Canada is comprised mainly of judges appointed by former Prime Ministers Trudeau and Mulroney. If there were a single policy issue to which both prime ministers agreed it would be bilingualism. It would be naive to think that they did not appoint a judicial panel that shared their federalist view of Canada and would offer support thereof. In that regard, the courts have gone well beyond legal minimalism, hence fulfilling the Canadian dream of a bilingual state, at least in terms of provisions for education.

7 Rights and Privileges to Denominational, Separate and Dissentient Schools

Introduction

At Confederation in 1867 education was delegated as a provincial responsibility.[1] Each province would be free to establish its own laws to define and govern education. As a result, the Parliament of Canada has no direct jurisdiction over education, except under section 93.[2]

Constitution Act 1867: Section 93

There were some limitations placed on provincial autonomy in legislating and administering education in respect to religion. Specifically, section 93(1), (2) and (3) of the *Constitution Act 1867* [formerly the *B.N.A. Act*] recognizes the continuance of the rights of denominational, separate and dissentient schools that existed at the time of Confederation, in some provinces. In fact, under section 93(4), the Governor-General in Council, and the federal Parliament serve in a remedial and supervisory role with respect to these same guarantees. Specifically, section 93 of the *Constitution Act 1867* states:

---

[1]   With the noted exceptions of education for Native Canadians, and educational services in penal institutions and in National Defence Schools -- as granted in 1867. In addition, the federal government theoretically has authority over education in the territories. In practice, however, the territories have autonomy in this regard.

[2]   See: *Ottawa Roman Catholic Separate School Trustees v. Ottawa* [1917] A.C. 76 (P.C.).

93.   In and for each Province the Legislature may exclusively make Laws in relation to Education, subject and according to the following Provisions:

(1)   Nothing in any such Law shall prejudicially affect any Right or Privilege with respect to Denominational Schools which any Class of Persons have by Law in the Province at the Union:

(2)   All the Powers, Privileges, and Duties at the Union by Law conferred and imposed in Upper Canada on the Separate Schools and School Trustees of the Queen's Roman Catholic Subjects shall be and the same are hereby extended to the Dissentient Schools of the Queen's Protestant and Roman Catholic Subjects in Québec:

(3)   Where in any Province a System of Separate or Dissentient Schools exists by Law at the Union or is thereafter established by the Legislature of the Province, an Appeal shall lie to the Governor General in Council from any Act or Decision of any Provincial Authority affecting any Right or Privilege of the Protestant or Roman Catholic Minority of the Queen's Subjects in relation to Education:

(4)   In case any such Provincial Law as from Time to Time seems to the Governor General in Council requisite for the due Execution of the Provisions of this Section is not made, or in case any Decision of the Governor General in Council on any Appeal under this Section is not duly executed by the proper Provincial Authority in that Behalf, then and in every such Case, and as far only as the Circumstances of each Case require, the Parliament of Canada may make remedial Laws for the due Execution of the Provisions of this Section and of any Decision of the Governor General in Council under this Section.

These provisions were made in 1867 when the original four

provinces joined the confederation, namely: New Brunswick, Nova Scotia, Ontario, and Québec. Modifications were made in regard to rights and privileges for denominational and separate schools for the provinces of Manitoba (1870), Alberta (1905), Saskatchewan (1905) and Newfoundland (1949) when they subsequently joined as provinces of Canada. Although the wording is somewhat lengthy, it is worth citing in its entirety to provide the reader with an accurate depiction of the status of educational religious rights in Canada at the time, and of course, today.

Rights and Privileges in Manitoba

Altered for Manitoba by section 22 of the *Manitoba Act 1870*, 33 Vict., c. 3 (Canada), (confirmed by the *Constitution Act 1871*), which reads as follows:

22.   In and for the Province, the said Legislature may exclusively make Laws in relation to Education, subject and according to the following provisions:—

(1)   Nothing in any such Law shall prejudicially affect any right or privilege with respect to Denominational Schools which any class of persons have by Law or practice in the Province at the Union:

(2)   An appeal shall lie to the Governor General in Council from any Act or decision of the Legislature of the Province, or of any Provincial Authority affecting any right or privilege, of the Protestant or Roman Catholic minority or the Queen's subjects in relation to Education:

(3)   In case any such Provincial Law, as from time to time seems to the Governor General in Council requisite for the due execution of the provisions of this section, is not made, or in case any decision of the Governor General in Council on any appeal under this section is not duly executed by the proper Provincial Authority in that behalf, then, and in every such case, and as far only as the

circumstances of each case require, the Parliament of Canada may make remedial Laws for the due execution of the provisions of this section, and of any decision of the Governor General in Council under this section.

Rights and Privileges in Alberta

Altered for Alberta by section 17 of the *Alberta Act,* 4-5 Edw. Vll, c. 3, 1905 (Canada), which reads as follows:

17.   Section 93 of the *Constitution Act 1867*, shall apply to the said province, with the substitution for paragraph (1) of the said section 93 of the following paragraph:

(1)   Nothing in any such law shall prejudicially affect any right or privilege with respect to separate schools which any class of persons have at the date of the passing of this Act, under the terms of chapters 29 and 30 of the Ordinances of the Northwest Territories, passed in the year 1901, or with respect to religious instruction in any public or separate school as provided for in the said ordinances.

(2)   In the appropriation by the Legislature or distribution by the Government of the province of any moneys for the support of schools organized and carried on in accordance with the said chapter 29 or any Act passed in amendment thereof, or in substitution therefor, there shall be no discrimination against schools of any class described in the said chapter 29.

(3)   Where the expression "by law" is employed in paragraph 3 of the said section 93, it shall be held to mean the law as set out in the said chapters 29 and 30, and where the expression "at the Union" is employed, in the said paragraph 3, it shall be held to mean the date at which this Act comes into force.

Rights and Privileges in Saskatchewan

Altered for Saskatchewan by section 17 of the *Saskatchewan Act, 4-5* Edw. Vll, c. 42, 1905 (Canada), which reads as follows:

17.   Section 93 of the *Constitution Act,* 1867, shall apply to the said province, with the substitution for paragraph (1) of the said section 93, of the following paragraph:

(1)   Nothing in any such law shall prejudicially affect any right or privilege with respect to separate schools which any class of persons have at the date of the passing of this Act, under the terms of chapters 29 and 30 of the Ordinances of the Northwest Territories, passed in the year 1901, or with respect to religious instruction in any public or separate school as provided for in the said ordinances.

(2)   In the appropriation by the Legislature or distribution by the Government of the province of any moneys for the support of schools organized and carried on in accordance with the said chapter 29, or any Act passed in amendment thereof or in substitution therefor, there shall be no discrimination against schools of any class described in the said chapter 29.

(3)   Where the expression "by law" is employed in paragraph (3) of the said section 93, it shall be held to mean the law as set out in the said chapters 29 and 30; and where the expression "at the Union" is employed in the said paragraph (3), it shall be held to mean the date which this Act comes into force.

Rights and Privileges in Newfoundland

Altered for Newfoundland by Term 17 of the *Terms of Union of Newfoundland with Canada* (confirmed by the *Newfoundland Act,* 12-13 Geo. Vl, c. 22 (U.K.)). Term 17 of the *Terms of Union of Newfoundland with Canada* set out in the Schedule to the *Newfoundland Act,* which was amended by the *Constitution Amendment 1987 (Newfoundland Act),* (see Sl/88-11) reads as follows:

17(1)   In lieu of section ninety-three of the *Constitution Act, 1867,* the following term shall apply in respect of the Province of Newfoundland:

In and for the Province of Newfoundland the Legislature shall have exclusive authority to make laws in relation to education, but the Legislature will not have authority to make laws prejudicially affecting any right or privilege with respect to denominational schools, common (amalgamated) schools, or denominational colleges, that any class or classes of persons have by law in Newfoundland at the date of Union, and out of public funds of the Province of Newfoundland, provided for education,

(a)   all such schools shall receive their share of such funds in accordance with scales determined on a non-discriminatory basis from time to time by the Legislature for all schools then being conducted under authority of the Legislature; and

(b)   all such colleges shall receive their share of any grant from time to time voted for all colleges then being conducted under authority of the Legislature, such grant being distributed on a non-discriminatory basis.

(2)   For the purposes of paragraph one of this Term, the Pentecostal Assemblies of Newfoundland have in Newfoundland all the same rights and privileges with respect to denominational schools and denominational colleges as any other class or classes of persons had by law in Newfoundland at the date of Union, and the words "all such schools" in paragraph *(a)* of paragraph one of this Term and the words "all such colleges" in paragraph *(b)* of paragraph one of this Term include, respectively, the schools and the colleges of the Pentecostal Assemblies of Newfoundland.

Recent Developments in Newfoundland

In a referendum held in September 1995 in the Province of Newfoundland, 54 per cent voted in favour of proposed Government reforms to end church control over education. Forty-six per cent were against such constitutional reforms, favouring the *status quo*. Although the Government claimed victory stating that the vote provides a mandate for reform, those against the proposed changes in education argue that it was a narrow win and thus the Government should re-open negotiations with the churches.

Premier Clyde Wells himself admitted that the "eight-point gap" between the for and against sides was "difficult to ignore". This is particularly important in view of the low voter turn-out (51.9 per cent). Proposed changes of this nature would involve Constitutional amendments under the *Terms of Union of Newfoundland with Canada,* which would have to be approved by Ottawa.

Following the referendum, the Well's Liberal Government stated it would move forward with proposed reform to institute ten inter-denominational school boards from the existing 27 denominational ones currently held by four Christian faiths. Church leaders fear that the proposed changes, which effectively whittle away their constitutional rights, is a Government attempt to secularize education in the Province. Government argue it is badly needed reform, as concluded by a 1992 Royal Commission. Moreover, they contend that such moves are based on fiscal responsibility and not a plot against Christian based schooling.

No Direct Federal Control over Education

Essentially, section 93, including the alterations pertaining to the provinces of Manitoba, Alberta, Saskatchewan and Newfoundland, delegates education as an "exclusively" provincial endeavour, with no direct federal control. Needless to say, there is indirect federal influence over education in that federal decisions invariably affect educational policies within individual provinces. All policy decisions relating to the public sector at large are inextricably linked as there is a seamless web between them. As a result, decisions in one area of federal decision-making are almost certain to spill into another, having an indirect impact, be it marginal or vast.

Federal decisions pertaining to immigration, for example, will indirectly affect provincial and school board educational policies. That is to say, federal immigration policies relating to admitting large numbers of non-English speaking individuals to Canada have indirectly affected school board decision-making in many large urban areas.[3]

Section 93 Protection

The conditions for claiming protection for section 93 rights and privileges are best summarized in the case of *Attorney General of Québec v. Lavigne* [1983] where Mr. Justice Chouinard states the conditions for claiming section 93 protection.

> In order to claim the protection of (s. 93), the following conditions must of necessity be met:
>
> (a)   there must be a right or privilege affecting a denominational school;
> (b)   enjoyed by a particular class of person;
> (c)   by law;
> (d)   in effect at the time of the Union;
> (e)   and which is prejudicially affected.

These protections of the rights and privileges owing to denominational and separate schools have been unaltered by the *Charter*. In fact, they have been enhanced by it.

---

3   Another example of indirect federal influence pertains to the amount of transfer payments granted to individual provinces. This sum undoubtedly affects the distribution and allocation of resources within public sector spending, education being a vulnerable area.

Constitution Act 1982: Section 29 of the *Charter*

Section 29 of the *Charter* reaffirms the constitutional provisions of section 93, stating that nothing in the *Charter* will "abrogate or derogate" from the denominational rights guaranteed at Confederation. That is to say, in light of other provisions in the *Charter* (e.g., equality rights and the guarantee of fundamental freedoms) each respective province must continue to respect the rights and privileges granted to these schools at Confederation. Section 29 of the *Charter* specifically states:

> 29.   Nothing in this Charter abrogates or derogates from any rights or privileges guaranteed by or under the Constitution of Canada in respect of denominational, separate or dissentient schools.

Denominational, Separate and Dissentient Schools Case Law

Section 29 of the *Charter* has sparked much controversy by religious minorities and individuals claiming inequitable treatment and discrimination. Cases typically involve issues pertaining to the funding of Roman Catholic schools in Ontario; denominational school rights and the rights of teachers; denominational school rights and taxation; denominational schools and minority language educational rights; and denominational and separate schools and freedom of religion and equality rights. Cases involving these issues are discussed in turn.

Funding Roman Catholic Schools in Ontario

Prior to the institution of the *Charter*, two important cases appeared before the courts, regarding section 93. In the end, neither the cases of *Tiny Separate School Trustees v. The King* [1928] nor *Attorney General of Québec v. Greater Hull School Board et al.* [1984], regarding Roman Catholic and Protestant minority denominational rights, respectively, were successful in furthering denominational causes. In *Tiny*, for example, the Privy Council ruled that Roman Catholic separate school funding need not be extended for all grade levels in Ontario secondary schools.

In 1986, however, the Ontario Government introduced Bill 30, allowing for full funding of Roman Catholic schools up to the end of secondary school. This decision was immediately challenged in the courts. The case of Bill 30 differed from the *Tiny* case, however, because it was now a Government decision to provide full funding to Roman Catholic schools. The Court challenge regarding the constitutionality of this provincial Government decision set denominational rights against fundamental freedoms and equality rights. This case, *Re Metropolitan Toronto Board of Education et al. v. Attorney General for Ontario* (1987) was ultimately decided by the Supreme Court of Canada.[4]

The principal questions at hand were whether the Ontario Legislature had the right to pass Bill 30, thus expanding the constitutionally protected denominational rights of Roman Catholics, and whether Bill 30 was immunized from the *Charter*. The Supreme Court ruled that, in 1867, Ontario separate schools did have the right to provide publicly funded education beyond the elementary level. In so doing, the Supreme Court of Canada effectively overruled the Privy Council decision in the *Tiny* case. In reaching its decision, the Supreme Court deemed it unnecessary to answer all the issues in question. Specifically, it did not rule on whether Bill 30 violated section 2(a) freedom of conscience and religion, or section 15(1) equality rights under the *Charter*. Nor, obviously, did the Court find it necessary to consider the application of section 1 of the *Charter* in this case.

Although the Court did not answer the issues central to section

---

[4]   It must be noted that there are varying points of view on the issue of funding religious schools. At the risk of over simplifying their respective arguments, the author will attempt to describe the essence of the various arguments. At the time of the extension of full funding to Roman Catholic schools, the Anglican Bishop of Toronto opposed the move arguing that Catholic schools should not be given further special advantage, essentially favouring the then existing public schools with *de jure* Christian teachings. The Dutch Reformed (Alliance of Christian Schools) case accepts Roman Catholic funding by the *Constitution Act* but argues that non-Catholic Christians should not be discriminated against. By this argument, the Roman Catholics did not have an historical privilege; in fact, in 1867 there were Roman Catholic and Protestant public schools; the discrimination against Protestants is new. The Jewish argument is different again. It essentially depends on American church/state separation and argues for funding of the secular part of Jewish education; this argument is inconsistent with the Dutch Reformed case. Evidently, these cases are more complex than this, but suffice it to say that the gist of their arguments have been presented.

2(a) and section 15(1), it did uphold Bill 30. Madam Justice Wilson stated that the rights and privileges guaranteed under section 93 are "immune from *Charter* review under section 29 of the *Charter*". She said that section 93 represents "a fundamental part of the Confederation compromise" and even without section 29 of the *Charter*, section 93 would stand. Hence, Bill 30, providing full funding for Roman Catholic separate high schools in the Province of Ontario, was ruled constitutionally valid.[5]

Denominational School Rights and Pre-Marital Sex and Catholic Dogma

The courts have decided that denominational schools have autonomy over issues involving community morals and religious doctrine. In *Casagrande v. Hinton Roman Catholic District No. 155 et al.* (1987) a female teacher who was pregnant was dismissed on denominational grounds. She was alleged to have engaged in pre-marital sexual intercourse, behaviour which clearly offends Roman Catholic teachings and doctrine. Casagrande argued, however, that she was dismissed from her duties because she was pregnant which was not a denominational cause but rather discrimination on the basis of sex, and hence contrary to section 15 of the *Charter*. The School Board argued that the fact that Casagrande was pregnant was not the reason for her dismissal but simply served as proof that she had engaged in pre-marital sexual relations.

     The Court accepted the Board's argument and agreed the teacher's conduct provided legitimate grounds for dismissal because it contravened Catholic doctrine. The fact that Casagrande was pregnant merely served as proof of her pre-marital practices and was not discrimination based on sex. The Court upheld the Board's decision to promote the level of morality it felt was necessary in keeping with the moral purposes of Catholic education.[6]

     In reaching its decision, the Court reviewed earlier decisions

---

5   Under Bill 30 separate school boards are permitted to discriminate in the hiring of Catholic teachers. This right expires in 1996.

6   See the next section for a case dealing with issues of morality in non-denominational schools.

regarding denominational issues.   Specifically, the Court examined *Re: Essex County Roman Catholic Separate School Board and Porter* [1978], where the Board was found to be within its jurisdiction in dismissing two teachers for entering civil marriages.   Also, the Court looked at the ruling in *Caldwell v. Stuart* [1984] where it was held that denominational cause was an appropriate reason for teacher dismissal.   In *Caldwell*, the Board's decision not to renew a Catholic teacher's teaching contract because of her civil service marriage to a divorced man, was upheld by the Supreme Court of Canada.   In that particular case, the Court stated that, "the requirement of religious conformance including the acceptable observance of the Church's rules regarding marriage is reasonable and necessary to assume the objectives of the school".

The Court stated, in the *Casagrande* decision, that denominational rights include "all rights and powers necessary to maintain the denominational character of such schools, and more specifically included the right to dismiss teachers for denominational causes".   The right to establish separate schools was granted by the Ordinances of the Northwest Territories and preserved by section 17 of the *Alberta Act 1905*.   The Court added: "it is clear that section 29 reaffirms and continues the constitutional rights granted in respect of denominational schools, giving these rights precedence over the individual rights protected by the other provisions of the *Charter*".

Issues of Morality in Non-Denominational Schools

Although this chapter focuses on issues involving denominational and separate schools, the present case from a non-denominational school is discussed as a matter of interest to the reader.   It is placed here purely out of convenience as it does not involve denominational schools.   The case of *Shewan v. Abbotsford School District 34* (1987) involved issues of morality, teacher conduct and ethics within a non-denominational setting.

Mrs. Shewan posed semi-nude for a photograph which subsequently appeared in a national "girlie" magazine.   The caption of the photograph gave reference to her being a Canadian teacher.   When news of the publication was released in the community at large Abbotsford School Board decided to suspend Mr. and Mrs. Shewan for misconduct (pursuant to section 122(1) of the *School Act*). The British Columbia Court of Appeal examined the meaning of the term "misconduct" within the context of the incident.

The Shewans argued that it was within their private interests to act as they saw fit. Mr. Shewan stated that the purpose of having his wife appear semi-nude in the magazine was to increase her self esteem. The Court consequently agreed with the School Board's decision to suspend Mr. and Mrs. Shewan for reasons of misconduct. The Court did, however, rule that the period of six weeks without pay initially decided by the Board was too harsh, reversing it to that of four weeks instead.

Dismissal, Denominational School Rights and the Rights of Teachers

The theme of section 29 taking precedence over all sections of the *Charter* is reiterated in the case of the *Newfoundland Teachers' Association and Walsh v. H. M. The Queen in Right of Newfoundland et al.* (1988). The Newfoundland Court of Appeal upheld the rights pertaining to denominational schools, with regard to teacher dismissal, as guaranteed in section 29 of the *Charter*. The Court stated that these rights generally outweigh individual religious freedoms, which go against or impair the right of the School Board.

Walsh, who had been hired by the respondent Board was a practising Roman Catholic at the time of his instatement in 1982. He later joined the Church of the Salvation Army, subsequently marrying a women of that same church. The Catholic School Board immediately moved to terminate Walsh's teaching contract. The Board maintained the dismissal was with just cause. Walsh (and the Newfoundland Teachers' Association) launched an unsuccessful grievance heard by an Arbitration Board. Walsh appealed to the Newfoundland Court of Appeal to set aside the Arbitration Board's decision (the dismissal). The Court dismissed the application, upholding the Catholic School Board's decision to terminate the teaching contract.[7]

---

7   Leave to appeal to the Supreme Court of Canada was refused.

Dismissal, Denominational School Rights and Tax Assignment

In the case of *Black v. Metropolitan Separate School Board* (1988) the plaintiff's termination of employment from a Catholic separate school board was upheld by the judiciary. Black had taught for many years with the Metropolitan Toronto Separate School Board but resigned to give birth to her first child. Up until 1982 she had directed her taxes to that Separate Board. At this time she re-directed her taxes to the Public Board to enrol her child in a nearby junior kindergarten programme with that Board.

In 1986, Black resumed her teaching duties, as a probationary teacher, with Metropolitan Separate School Board. At this time she was informed of the Board's policy that required teachers to direct their taxes to the Separate Board. Black did not comply with this policy and was consequently fired for not directing her taxes to the Metropolitan Separate School Board. She claimed that her being fired violated her rights pursuant to section 15, equality, section 2(a), freedom of conscience and religion, and section 7, life, liberty and security of the person, under the *Charter*.

The Supreme Court of Ontario dismissed these *Charter* arguments stating that the Board had the right to request her taxes. Firstly, the Court rejected the argument that since Metropolitan Separate School Board was the only board in the province that had such a policy it constituted discrimination under section 15. The Court stated that all boards of education are distinct and can have different policies.

Secondly, the Board policy did not put Black at a disadvantage and did not interfere with her choice of education for her child, therefore there was no violation of her religious freedom.

Thirdly, there was no evidence that the board policy regarding taxes violated the principles of fundamental justice. It did not dictate the type of religious education the child was to receive and it did not place economic hardship on the parents. The Board had the right to require teachers to direct their taxes thereto.

Property Owners are Required to Pay School Taxes

Another case regarding the rights of separate schools and taxation was

Resort Village of Mitusinne v. Outlook School Division No. 32 (1989), in Saskatchewan. In this case, it was ruled that every property owner is required to pay school taxes. Only where separate schools exist are taxpayers allowed to select whether they prefer to have their taxes sent to the public or separate system. Section 29 of the *Charter* does not provide a "guaranteed right" that minority taxpayers will have their taxes directed only to separate schools.

Taxation, Religious Beliefs and Equality Rights

Another case involving taxes occurred in Newfoundland. A Provincial Court ruled in the case of *St. John's School Tax Authority v. Winter* (1990), that the defendant had to pay outstanding school tax arrears. The Court stated that he had to pay taxes, regardless of religious beliefs. Further, his ineligibility to stand for school board elections did not constitute discrimination within the meaning of section 15 of the *Charter*.

Denominational Schools and Minority Language Educational Rights

Although section 29 overrides fundamental freedoms, legal rights and equality rights guaranteed under the *Charter*, as was demonstrated in some of the cases presented throughout this chapter, section 23 is one area where section 29 rights are not directly affected. Minority language educational rights and the rights and privileges granted to denominational and separate schools can exist simultaneously.

In the case of *Griffin v. Commission Scolaire Regionale Blainville Deux-Montagnes et al.* (1989), (as discussed in Chapter Six on minority language educational rights) the Court decided that the group of English Roman Catholics are entitled to minority language educational facilities, but not to denominational minority language educational facilities. The *Charter* does not make express reference to the religious or denominational characteristics of minority language facilities. Nor does the *Charter* make reference to denominational control or management of such facilities.

Although there is no express reference in the *Charter* to provide for denominational minority language educational rights, there is no direct reference stating they cannot.   As a result, the courts will uphold provincial legislation to provide for these rights in provinces which currently have denominational systems.   In the 1984 Ontario *Reference* case, for example, the Court ruled that it was within the legislative authority of the Government of Ontario to provide for the election of minority language trustees to Roman Catholic separate school boards. Further, the trustees can exercise certain exclusive responsibilities dealing with the minority language sections within these boards.

Linguistic versus Religious Boundaries in Québec

By an Order-In-Council, the Québec Government asked the Québec Court of Appeal to determine whether certain provisions of the provincial *Education Act* violated section 93(1) and (2) of the *Constitution Act 1867*. The Court said yes to certain questions and no to others.   In *Reference Re: Education Act (Québec)* (1993), the Supreme Court of Canada, however, said no to all five questions.

These questions concerned the province's jurisdiction over legislative reform of education.   The five sets of questions were as follows:

1.   Does the *Education Act* (1988, c. 84), in particular ss. 111, 354, 519, 521, 522 and 527, prejudicially affect the rights and privileges protected by s. 93(1) and (2) of the Constitution Act, 1867 by providing for the establishment of French language and English language school boards which will succeed to the rights and obligations of school boards for Catholics and Protestants?

2.   Does the Education Act, in particular ss. 126 to 139 and 206, prejudicially affect the rights and privileges protected by s. 93(1) and (2) of the Constitution Act, 1867 in its provisions:

(a)   which stipulate the manner in which the right to dissent is to be exercised and the manner in which dissentient school boards are to be established;

(b)   which give the government the power to change the legal structures of the dissentient school boards and to terminate the existence of those which do not perform any of the functions contemplated in the Act;

(c) which restrict access to these school boards to persons who belong to the same religious denomination as that of these school boards?

3. Does the *Education Act*, in particular ss. 122, 123, 124, 206, 519, 521 and 522, prejudicially affect the rights and privileges protected by s. 93(1) and (2) of the Constitution Act, 1867:

(a) by continuing the existence of the confessional school boards in their territories;

(b) by allowing the government to change these territories;

(c) by providing for a means of transferring part of their rights and obligations to French language and English language school boards;

(d) by restricting access to these school boards to persons who belong to the same religious denomination as that of these school boards?

4. Does the Education Act, in particular ss. 423, 424, 425, 428 and 439, prejudicially affect the rights and privileges protected by s. 93(1) and (2) of the *Constitution Act, 1867* in that:

(a) it gives the Conseil scolaire de l'Ile de Montreal the power to borrow money on behalf of all school boards on the island of Montreal;

(b) it authorizes the Conseil scolaire to establish rules for apportioning the proceeds of the tax it collects on behalf of these school boards?

5. Does the *Education Act*, in particular ss. 49, 223, 227, 230, 261 and 568, prejudicially affect the rights and privileges protected by s. 93(1) and (2) of the *Constitution Act, 1867*, in that it gives the Catholic committee and the Protestant committee of the Conseil supérieur de l'éducation the authority:

(a)   to establish rules respecting the confessional nature of the schools of the confessional and dissentient school boards;

(b)   to approve the programs of studies for religious instruction offered in such schools and to determine the qualification of persons providing that instruction and those assigned to pastoral or religious care and guidance in such schools? (154 N.R. pp. 7-9)

In essence, the basic issue the Supreme Court addressed was whether the Québec Government could create a new non-denominational board system along linguistic lines. The new legislation (Bill 107) proposed to divide the province into two groups of territories: one for French language school boards and one for English language school boards. It did not, however, propose to dissolve the existing five dissentient (unless a dissentient school board became inactive) and four denominational school boards (it could alter the territory of denominational boards). By answering all five questions in the negative, the Supreme Court ruled that the legislative scheme did not amount to a breach of the rights guaranteed by section 93 of the *Constitution Act 1867*.

It should be noted, however, that the Education Minister of Québec, Pauline Marois, has recently announced that Roman Catholic and Protestant school boards will be completely replaced with French language and English language boards by mid-1998 (*Maclean's* (Weekly Magazine) 24 June 1996 at p. 21). The new system will allow Protestants and Catholics to set up special committees whereby they will be permitted to run some schools within these respective linguistic school boards.[8]

Denominational and Separate Schools: Freedom of Religion and Equality Rights

In *Adler v. Ontario* (1992), six parties brought forward the case that Ontario's full funding of Roman Catholic schools and not other religious-based schools or school systems, violated their *Charter* rights under section 2(a) and section 15. In *Re: Adler and The Queen* (1992), the

---

8   Needless to say, such a move will be met with court challenge.

Ontario Court (General Division) ruled that the funding of Roman Catholic schools and school systems, and not other religious-based schools and schools systems, constituted discrimination on the basis of religion under section 15 of the *Charter*. Further, mandatory attendance laws, concomitant with the non-funding of independent schools, infringed the guarantee of freedom of religion under section 2(a) of the *Charter*.

The Court stated, however, that the governmental policy of not funding other religious groups (other than Roman Catholics) was a reasonable limit under section 1 of the *Charter*. The decision not to fund other religions was reasonable in view of the fact that the legislative objective of providing a secular public education system in Ontario was pressing and substantial and the Government's policy was rationally connected to achieving this objective. The Court stated that, "the public funding of Roman Catholic separate schools in Ontario is a constitutional anomaly with its roots in a historic and political compromise made as an incident of Confederation" (p. 417, 94 D.L.R. (4th)).

In *Adler v. Ontario* (1994) the applicants took their case to the Ontario Court of Appeal. Once again they challenged the absence of public funding for the schools to which they sent their children. They claimed it amounted to violations of their freedom of religion (section 2) and their equality rights (section 15) under the *Charter*. They sought declarations to that effect (that their rights had been violated), as well as court orders to extend funding to their schools. The Court of Appeal dismissed the Appeal stating that, "the Ontario *Education Act*, and the school health support services legislation are consistent with *Constitution Act* 1982" (p. 38, 116 D.L.R. (4th)), hence there was no violation of the *Charter*.

In *Adler v. Ontario* (1997) the Supreme Court of Canada has since upheld the Court of Appeal ruling.[9] Chief Justice Lamer and Justices La Forest, Gonthier, Cory and Iacobucci stated:[10]

> Section 93 of the Constitution Act, 1867 is the product of a historical compromise crucial to Confederation and forms a comprehensive code with respect to denominational school rights

---

[9] McLachlin J. dissented in part and L'Heureux-Dube J. dissented.

[10] Quoted from unpublished documents of the Supreme Court of Canada rulings (File No.: 24347), pages 2-3 of 70.

which cannot be enlarged through the operation of s[ection] 2(a) of the *Charter*. It does not represent a guarantee of fundamental freedoms. The appellants, given that they cannot bring themselves within the terms of s[ection] 93's guarantees, have no claim to public funding for their schools. To decide otherwise by accepting the appellants' claim that s[ection] 2(a) requires public funding of their religion-based independent schools would be to hold one section of the Constitution violative of another.

Section 93(1) requires the Ontario government to fund Roman Catholic separate schools fully. The claim that the government's choice to fund Roman Catholic schools contravened the equality provisions of s[ection] 15(1) of the *Charter* should be rejected for two reasons. First, the decision falls fairly and squarely within s[ection] 29 of the *Charter* which explicitly exempts from *Charter* challenge all rights and privileges guaranteed under the Constitution in respect of denominational, separate or dissentient schools. Second, the decision is nonetheless immune from *Charter* review because it was made pursuant to the plenary power in relation to education granted to provincial legislatures as part of the Confederation compromise. One part of the Constitution cannot be used to interfere with rights protected by a different part of that same document.

In addition, the Supreme Court stated that in order to claim protection under section 93, "it must be shown that there was a right or privilege with respect to denominational schooling which was enjoyed by a class of persons by law at the time of union".

[Moreover], [t]he province remains free to exercise its plenary power with regard to education in whatever way it sees fit, subject to the restrictions relating to separate schools imposed by s[ection] 93(1). The province's legislative power is not limited to the public and Roman Catholic school systems. However, legislation in respect of education could be subject to *Charter* scrutiny whenever the government decides to go beyond the confines of this special mandate to fund Roman Catholic separate public schools.

Élitist Tendencies in Judicial Rulings: Denominational Schools

There is little doubt that section 29 of the *Charter* reaffirms rights guaranteed under section 93 of the *Constitution Act* 1867 regarding denominational, separate and dissentient schools. Indeed, the judiciary upholds that such rights alone were guaranteed at Confederation, and thus do not compete with *Charter* guarantees. One part of the *Constitution* cannot be used to cancel another unless the *Constitution* so provides.

Although section 29 of the *Charter* reaffirms the rights allotted to these school systems, according to the Supreme Court, this section is not necessary to uphold section 93 rights. These rights survive by virtue of their constitutional guarantee alone, without the aid of the *Charter*. Recognition under section 29 of the *Charter* serves as a reaffirmation, but one that is not really necessary because the existing constitutional guarantees themselves are sufficiently strong.

Court rulings on issues relating to section 29 follow the political ideology that a constitutional guarantee made in 1867, as part of the Confederation bargain, cannot be invalidated some one hundred and fifteen years later (the time of the ruling in the Bill 30 case) under section 15. Courts recognize that such endeavours would take constitutional reform (see *Adler*) on the part of politicians and not judicial activism. The judiciary is not willing to utilize its perceived role and overstep the dominant political ideology of the day which supports a protected religious system within an otherwise secular state, and alongside a secular educational system (as per the rulings of *Zylberberg*, *Russow* and *Elgin*).

It is evident that at the time of drafting the *Charter*, and still today, federal political players in the inner circle of decision-making supported the notion and the continuance of the rights and privileges of these systems protected under section 93. If not, they would never have included section 29 in the *Charter*. At best it would have been left open to interpretation without reaffirming such rights within the *Charter*. In addition, the political decision to extend funding in Ontario Catholic schools indicates a validation of the notion of a religious school system, at least in the Province of Ontario. As evidenced from the Bill 30 case, and reaffirmed most recently in *Adler*, the Supreme Court of Canada is willing to accept this decision and not strike it down as a violation of equality and religious rights, as some groups would like to have happened.

There appears to be some ambiguity in that on the one hand, the Government of Ontario support a secular school system (see *Zylberberg*, *Bal* and *Elgin*), whilst on the other hand, they support a religious system parallel thereto. As to the reasoning behind such an ideology, it is left mainly to conjecture. Perhaps it is politically wise to support a Catholic system when at the time of the decision to extend full funding to denominational schools (under Bill 30), percentage-wise over half of the population of the Province claimed to be Catholic. Perhaps it was to rectify an injustice that was created in the *Tiny* ruling when the notion of extending full funding was lost in a challenge in 1928.

Regardless of the reasoning behind the policy decision to support denominational education within Ontario, and the federal and provincial governments' obvious support by including section 29 in the *Charter*, these decisions mark a dominant political ideology which supports religious rights and privileges guaranteed at Confederation. Further, the Supreme Court of Canada is willing to uphold this political choice. In the case of Bill 30, it effectively overturned the Privy Council decision of 1928 in *Tiny* stating the Council had erred in its judgement.

In essence, the Supreme Court has assumed a role which galvanizes political ideology into social and legal reality for denominational schools. Provincial courts have signalled similar support in decisions such as *Casagrande* and *Black*. It will be interesting to see what will evolve in relation to the recent moves to change the educational systems in Québec and Newfoundland.

On the one hand the judiciary say that minority groups can no longer be subjected to the "tyranny" of the Christian majority (as per political ideology in the cases of *Zylberberg*, *Russow* and *Elgin*) whilst on the other hand, they state that the religious systems protected under section 93 are sacred and cannot be touched. What is more, those working within such systems must adhere strictly to Catholic dogma (see *Casagrande*). The only apparent consistency in these rulings is the support of the political will of the day, which is at present supporting Confederationally-entrenched denominational school systems parallel to those of modern day secular ones.

Denominational School Conclusion

The judiciary is offering conservative interpretations when *Charter* challenges involve denominational and separate schools. Judges are maintaining the *status quo* of rights and privileges protected under section 93 of the *Constitution Act 1867*, and affirmed under section 29 of the *Charter*. The courts are ruling in accordance with the provisions of the *Constitution Act*, 1867, which acknowledge denominational and separate school systems. These school systems are recognized by the courts as compromises upon which Canada was founded, even though the principle of such rulings may appear to be at odds with broader notions of equality within a supposed egalitarian society.

Needless to say, for some religious minorities such historical and political compromises sit uncomfortably with their notions of equality rights and religious freedoms within the *Charter*. They contend that denominational and separate schools enjoy "élitist" privileges which serve to protect and actually expand the rights of the people supporting such systems.[11] Nevertheless, in the Bill 30 case in Ontario, the Supreme Court of Canada made it explicitly clear that religious systems protected under section 93 and affirmed under section 29 are untouchable (see also *Adler*). They are not willing to unravel what they see as the very fabric of Canadian society, regardless of how unjust such a stand may seem to some.

---

[11]   With the institution of such religious educational systems, they were not at the time privileges but merely an expression of the education systems that developed to represent those social systems. They become "privileges" only when legislatures and the courts freeze the existing rights (or in the case of Ontario, expand them) whilst refusing to grant equivalent rights to other minorities similar to those granted schools in 1867.

8   Multiculturalism and the Rights of Aboriginal Peoples

Introduction

In recent years issues pertaining to multiculturalism and the rights of aboriginal peoples have taken more prominence on political agendas. Much emphasis has been placed on full participation of all Canadians within society, regardless of their ethnic or cultural heritage. The following chapter discusses issues pertaining to both multiculturalism (Section I) and aboriginal rights (Section II) under the *Charter*. These two topics are placed together in the same chapter solely out of convenience and not because they are deemed inseparable. In addition, there is no discussion of case law under either of these topics. The wording of the *Charter* is presented for each of these topics followed by an ideological discussion relating to each.

Section I: The *Charter* and Multiculturalism

The *Canadian Charter* enhances the ethnocultural heritage of all Canadians. It extends rights to minority peoples, in at least three ways. Firstly, under section 15(1) it sets out that all Canadians are equal before and under the law, regardless of their ethnicity (as discussed in Chapter Five: Equality Rights). Secondly, under section 2(a) it guarantees freedom of religion and belief to all Canadians, regardless of the nature of their beliefs, Christian or otherwise (as discussed in Chapter Three: Fundamental Freedoms). Thirdly, the *Charter* expressly states that any interpretation of *Charter* laws must be consistent with the multicultural nature of Canada. Specifically, section 27 states:

> This *Charter* shall be interpreted in a manner consistent with the preservation and enhancement of the multicultural heritage of Canadians.

The Canadian *Multicultural Act*

Concomitant to the 1982 enactment of the *Charter*, on 12 July 1988, the House of Commons passed an Act (Bill C-93) for "the preservation and enhancement of multiculturalism in Canada". The relevant portions of the Act state:

> It is hereby declared to be the policy of the Government of Canada to:
>
> (a) recognize and promote the understanding that multiculturalism reflects the cultural and racial diversity of Canadian society and acknowledges the freedom of all members of Canadian society to preserve, enhance and share their cultural heritage;
>
> (b) recognize and promote the understanding that multiculturalism is a fundamental characteristic of the Canadian heritage and identity and that it provides an invaluable resource in the shaping of Canada's future;
>
> (c) promote the full and equitable participation of individuals and communities of all origins in the continuing evolution and shaping of all aspects of Canadian society and assist them in the elimination of any barrier to such participation;
>
> (d) recognize the existence of communities whose members share a common origin and their historic contribution to Canadian society, and enhance their development;
>
> (e) ensure that all individuals receive equal treatment and equal protection under the law, while respecting and valuing their diversity;
>
> (f) encourage and assist the social, cultural, economic and political institutions of Canada to be both respectful and inclusive of Canada's multicultural character;
>
> (g) promote the understanding and creativity that arise from the interaction between individuals and communities of different origins;
>
> (h) foster the recognition and appreciation of the diverse cultures of Canadian society and promote the reflection

and the evolving expressions of those cultures;

(i)   preserve and enhance the use of languages other than English and French, while strengthening the status and use of the official languages of Canada; and

(j)   advance multiculturalism throughout Canada in harmony with the national commitment to the official languages of Canada.

In essence, Bill C-93 specifies, as public policy, measures to be taken to ensure a multicultural state, whilst the *Charter* galvanizes these principles into constitutional law.

Preserving and Promoting Multiculturalism

The *Charter* has been an important force in preserving and promoting multiculturalism and expanding the rights of students from minority backgrounds. There have been changes in a number of policies and practices that can be directly (and indirectly) attributed to the *Charter of Rights and Freedoms*. There is an increased sensitivity given to issues relating to inclusionary practices that focus on the needs of all students, regardless of ethnic, linguistic or religious background. In fact, raising the level of awareness towards multiculturalism and the pluralistic nature of Canada has become very politicized under the *Charter* and the *Multicultural Act*. Discriminatory practices are increasingly taboo, for fear of legal suits.

Awareness: An Increased Focus on Multiculturalism in Schools

Most schools have witnessed a marked increase in the interest given to multiculturalism in recent years. Initiatives have been taken to institute at least some component of multiculturalism into everyday routines and practices in schools, be it through the changing of prayers at opening exercises or through a re-focusing of teaching content and learning objectives. It is well accepted that the *Charter* is a catalyst for such change.

Although the *Charter* may not be the only impetus for an increased awareness of multiculturalism, it has been both indirectly (symbolically) as well as directly (legally)[1] responsible for policy changes. As a result, multicultural awareness has become a "strong force" in many schools, occupying staff development time and finding its way to the agendas of school board meetings.

Changes in Curriculum and Pedagogy

The biggest impact has been on curriculum and pedagogy (what is taught and how it is taught).   Paradigm shifts in curriculum development and programme delivery are commonplace.   Traditional course content has come under increased scrutiny as being exclusionary to some students, and in some instances has been deemed racist.   For example, educators have become more sensitive about which novels and books they use in their classes.   The essentially traditional, Christian and Eurocentric values of literature in school programmes are being replaced by books representing a variety of values and ideologies, with strong Christian books being eliminated.   Some "classical" works have been banned from schools because of derogatory comments that, in effect, marginalize students. Many works are increasingly under scrutiny because of their "unacceptable" ideology, e.g., *Huckleberry Finn*, *Merchant of Venice*, *Othello* and all of Jane Austen's works.[2]

Promoting Non-Traditional Teaching Methodologies

Attention has been drawn to the notion of values and the imposition of one's views on others.   Input is being sought from educators who may in the past have been ostracized for promoting unpopular teaching methods and materials (namely teachers of minority backgrounds).   As a result, course content and teaching methodologies that were not used in the past

---

[1]   In particular, see the discussion on changes relating to religious-based curriculum and opening school exercises as discussed in Chapter Three: Fundamental Freedoms.

[2]   Ironically, the works of Austen have enjoyed recent media success with cinema and television adaptations of several of her novels.

because they did not represent a dominant Anglo-European perspective, have since become acceptable, and indeed popular. In other words, education no longer solely promotes a mainstream Anglo culture that marginalizes minority views. In fact, it encourages them. Some boards of education actively promote February as African-American month, for example, featuring the literary works of black authors and pinnacling African-American inventions and achievements.

Restructuring and Integrated Subject Approaches

The new focus in curriculum design is on producing innovative and creative learning centres which effectively promote and foster a greater awareness of all people, from all cultural backgrounds. Many of these initiatives involve integrated subject approaches. Ontario, in particular, reports a complete restructuring effort to de-stream Grade 9, in an effort to be more equitable and to not type-cast certain students as academic or non-academic, in part, based on socio-economics or ethnic background and socialization. Such initiatives focus on changing curriculum content as well as teaching pedagogy.

Conventional methods of delivery and teaching styles are continually questioned, throughout Canada. Teachers are trying to address the needs of all students. The traditional notion of the teacher standing in front of the class and lecturing to students sitting in rows whilst they correct their homework and prepare for the next round of seat-work is increasingly shunned. Teachers are encouraged to be more responsive to the learning styles of "all" students.

School boards are encouraging excellence in teaching practices which break down barriers which are thought to exclude certain students from developing to their fullest academic potential. A number of new courses have been instituted into school programmes, as well as independent study programmes, where students are encouraged to develop their own area of expertise within a given subject. In essence, teacher-directed learning is no longer the sole means of subject content transmission. Once again, although not all of these changes are directly attributed to the *Charter*, a great deal of this re-thinking can be so attributed.

Central Ambiguity in Multiculturalism: Acculturalism

There is a central ambiguity in the meaning of multiculturalism.   If everyone has to accept one set of values to succeed, say for example, the set of values which the Government is currently embracing in schools, (secularism, bilingualism, environmentalism and equality), the author contends that it will effectively mean the end of multiculturalism in its true form.   More appropriately, it will be what the author would call "acculturalism", that is one set of values (secular;   bilingual; environmentally aware, embracing the motto to re-cycle, re-use and reduce;   and, equal, focusing on co-operation and collaboration as opposed to competitiveness).

Some argue that valuing different cultures means permitting parents to choose different school cultures for their children -- religious, linguistic, or otherwise.   But multiculturalism in Canada is a political decision (supported by the symbolic effect of the *Charter* and reinforced by the courts under section 2 and section 15) for ideologically political correct minorities to impose a single secular belief system by removing traditional Western, Judeo-Christian beliefs and symbols.

On a policy level, notions of equality sound very comforting. But many school principals and experts question the pragmatics of many of these symbolic gestures (see Black-Branch, 1993a).   They question whether, in the end, minority parents will want their children being taught by people from their own communities. It would seem, superficially, that they would. A teacher may be more empathetic and aware of the needs of a child, from the same cultural background, and thus bring certain understandings that will enhance the child's education. But, pragmatically speaking, one could question whether minority parents will want, for example, their children being taught to read by people who have a "heavy ethnic accent" or those with a "severe learning disability".   Under the *Charter*, "everyone" is equal and factors such as "accent" and "disability" do not constitute a basis for discrimination, but most school boards want the most "effective" teachers in their schools and most parents would likely prefer the "best" teacher available, irrespective of race, gender or ethnicity.

Multiculturalism Conclusion:
Political Élitism and the Empowerment of the Minority

In summary, in recent years there have been substantial changes in policy and practice which favour a multicultural perspective. Changes in curriculum content and teaching approaches aim to be more inclusive for all students, regardless of their ethnicity. Such changes have invariably been proposed and supported by the political *status quo,* which favours a multicultural Canada.

In the final analysis, it seems that the *Charter* has both created, and indeed fosters, a certain rights consciousness that inevitably empowers minority children in regard to education. This empowerment may, in part, be attributed to three factors. Firstly, the 1982 enactment of the *Canadian Charter of Rights and Freedoms* protects basic rights and freedoms under constitutional law. Secondly, more people have become aware of their rights in recent years. Thirdly, more people are claiming their rights.

As a result Canada has moved more into the domain of being a rights-conscious society in which individuals increasingly assert their rights. This empowerment of cultural, linguistic and religious minorities has infiltrated school settings, fostering notions of equality for all Canadians. It seems that the politically driven notion of the multicultural mosaic of the 1960s and 1970s is no longer just a concept, it is now being played out as constitutional law. What better place to sow such seeds than in educational institutions where impressionable young minds will espouse these broader principles of equality within an egalitarian society. Multiculturalism effectively aims to level class hierarchy based on race.

Section II: Aboriginal Rights and the *Charter*

Amid the fanfare, pomp and circumstance owing to the signing of the *Canada Act 1982*, the future impact for aboriginal peoples[3] was largely disregarded. Today, most aboriginal peoples would say that the *Charter* has done very little regarding change in the area of education. In essence, they feel the *Charter* maintains the political *status quo*.

Rights and Freedoms of Aboriginal Peoples

Whilst it may indeed be true, that the *Charter* does maintain the political *status quo,* it does, in fact, provide for aboriginal issues. Section 25 of the *Charter* states:

> The guarantee in this Charter of certain rights and freedoms shall not be construed so as to abrogate or derogate from any aboriginal, treaty or other rights and freedoms that pertain to the aboriginal peoples of Canada including:
> (a)   any rights or freedoms that have been recognized by the Royal Proclamation of October 7, 1763; and
> (b)   any rights or freedoms that may be acquired by the aboriginal peoples of Canada by way of land claims settlement.

Existing Rights of Aboriginal Peoples

Part II of the *Constitution Act 1982* also provides for the existing rights of aboriginal peoples. Section 35 states:

---

3   It should be noted for the purposes of this discussion that: (1) Indians and land reserved for Indians are a concern exclusively reserved for the federal Government (as per section 91(24) *Constitution Act* 1867); (2) "Indians" for the purposes of section 91 includes Inuit although Inuit are not "Indians" for the purposes of the *Indian Act* (see *Re: Eskimos*); and, (3) "aboriginal peoples" includes Indians, Inuit, and Métis.

35(1) The existing aboriginal and treaty rights of aboriginal peoples of Canada are hereby recognized and affirmed.

(2)   In this Act, "aboriginal peoples of Canada" includes the Indian, Inuit and Métis peoples of Canada.

One must bear in mind that section 35 (Part II) is not part of the *Charter*, whereas section 25 is a component thereof.

The *Charter* as Law

The *Canadian Charter of Rights and Freedoms* undoubtedly opens the school house gate to legal scrutiny. Well over 200 education related cases have been heard by the courts since the institution of the *Charter* in 1982. As evidenced in this book, legal arguments typically involve issues of fundamental freedoms, legal rights, equality rights, minority language education rights, and denominational and separate schools rights. These judicial decisions are not likely to have any direct impact on aboriginal education, however.

These cases involved neither aboriginal peoples nor aboriginal issues. In sum, aboriginal individuals and activists wanting educational change are not using the *Charter,* within judicial fora, as a means of challenging school policies and practices. At first glance, this finding may not appear significant but, in fact, it is because it raises many important questions as to why aboriginal individuals and groups have not used the *Charter* as a vehicle for educational reform, like so many others.

Section 25 Maintains the *Status Quo*

Generally speaking, the *Charter* has done very little to improve the conditions of education for Aboriginal Peoples. In fact, there is a marked irony that many individuals and groups have benefited from the *Charter* (within the educational context) whilst aboriginal peoples, who have obvious legal arguments, have not. Section 25 has done, and it seems will do, little to expand or even protect the rights of aboriginal peoples, in any sector of society. It seems that this provision was a symbolic inclusion and means very little, if anything.

Aboriginal Self-Governance is the Key to Change

Since 1982, there seems to be more political and popular will to resolve some of the long-standing issues pertaining to aboriginal self-governance, unlike a decade ago with the signing of the *Canada Act*. The *Charlottetown Agreement 1992*, for example, was to offer aboriginal self-government. Most importantly, it was drafted with participation from the Governments of Canada and delegations representing aboriginal peoples, including the Assembly of First Nations, the Inuit Tapirisat of Canada, the Native Council of Canada and the Métis National Council.

Specifically, the draft legal text of the failed *Agreement,* was to recognize that, "the Aboriginal peoples of Canada have the inherent right to self-government within Canada" (section 35.1). Included in this right was the right "to safeguard and develop their languages, cultures, economies, identities, institutions and traditions" (section 35.1(3a)). The constitutional entrenchment of these rights would have had profound implications regarding the management, control and governance of education within the scope of aboriginal self-governance.

It seems that this may come through negotiations for land claim settlements and as part of aboriginal self-government. Many experts offering commentary on issues concerning education and aboriginal peoples say that the *Charter* itself has done very little to bring forth change. Similarly, it is highly unlikely that education related *Charter* case law would expand the rights of aboriginal peoples. It is safe to say that the *Charter* maintains the *status quo* for aboriginal peoples in most sectors of society and education is no different. Changes of any magnitude appear tied to future constitutional negotiations regarding self-government and the settling of land claims.

Whilst the *Charlottetown Agreement* gave promise of change, many aboriginal leaders, and politicians alike, were gravely disappointed with the "No" vote on the constitutional referendum and thus the failure of the *Agreement*. Hopes for change in all sectors of aboriginal affairs, including education were riding on the *Agreement*. In the mean time, issues of equality and the education of aboriginal peoples will continue to be politically contentious.[4]

Conclusion: The Élitist Paradox Regarding Aboriginal Education

Perhaps one of the reasons why the *Charter* has not been instrumental in advancing the plight of aboriginal peoples within the educational context is because of the lack of consensus on how to actually "improve" the situation for aboriginal peoples. As a result there is no over-arching political agenda to guide those affecting change. The élite political ideology is left rather ambiguous, unlike areas such as minority language rights or the secularization of non-denominational schools, where there is a clear direction.

Specifically, whilst it is true that there is more popular and political support regarding aboriginal issues than there has been in the past, it is also true that the means by which the political élite seek to "improve" the situation soon becomes a quagmire of good intentions which inadvertently complicate the situation further. The prevailing view is that improvement will evolve by firstly, enhancing the chances of aboriginal students to participate in mainstream economic life, and secondly, by increasing cultural and administrative autonomy of Aboriginal schools. Whilst at first sight these ends in themselves seem easy enough to accomplish, upon deeper analysis it becomes evident that they are mutually exclusive of one another. Thus there is a paradox regarding the direction for improving aboriginal education.

The two stated goals are incompatible in that by increasing the level of autonomy under self-governed schools within a self-regulated educational system for aboriginal peoples, there is less likelihood of actually increasing aboriginal participation within mainstream economic life. In fact, it serves to further marginalize aboriginal peoples. The more autonomy they acquire, the less integrated into the mainstream they become. And *vice versa*, the more integrated into the mainstream

---

[4]   For further discussion on aboriginal issues see: Black-Branch, J. L. (1993c) O'Canada, Our Home on Native Land: Aboriginal Self Government May Be the Key to Educational Reform Not the Charter of Rights and Freedoms, *The Canadian Journal of Native Studies*, Vol. 13, No. 2.

aboriginal peoples become, the less political autonomy they harbour. This may account for some of the difficulties currently hindering progress on aboriginal issues, not just in regard to education but within other sectors of society as well. That is, whilst well-intended, the political élites are unsuccessfully pushing an agenda that is systematically flawed by its very nature. As a result, ambiguity remains and thus there is a lack of political consensus as to the precise direction aboriginal education should take. After all, the politically élite cannot march in two directions at once, that is having autonomy and full economic participation simultaneously, hence there is little progress, and much frustration, for the aboriginal peoples as a minority group within Canada (unlike for others, namely, minority language rightholders and religious minorities in non-denominational schools).

In other words, the political sentiment of the day may at this point appear to be the good intention of settling aboriginal issues (as per the *Charlottetown Agreement*) but, the reality is that there is a lack of political resolve to actually carry these intentions through. As a result, at the end of the day these issues linger and no great movement is made toward settling the aboriginal question.

9 Conclusion: The Politicization of the Courts

Introduction

Since 1982 the *Charter* has been a catalyst for a flurry of court activity in the domain of education, resulting in wide-scale scrutiny of educational policy and practice. Whilst judicial decisions in some of these cases have had an immediate impact on particular schools, others have profound implications for schools and schools systems across Canada. Areas typically litigated include issues of fundamental freedoms; legal rights; equality rights; minority language education rights; and, denominational, separate and dissentient schools rights.

The Impact of Litigation in Education

Litigation, on the one hand, is serving to bring about some liberal changes in certain areas of education hence re-aligning school systems. Many of these are having profound implications for educational policy. Other judicial rulings, on the other hand, serve to maintain and, in effect, reinforce the political *status quo*. Some rulings have strengthened the rights of minorities to increase their control over the education of their children. This is particularly true of the francophone linguistic minority outside of Québec. At the same time, the courts have helped to oversee the elimination of traditional Protestant education (particularly in public schools in Ontario and British Columbia) without permitting redress for dissenting minorities, of Protestant and other religions alike. Other rulings have directly strengthened the control of the educational bureaucracies, in the areas of programme and school discipline.

Important rulings such as *Jones* support the larger framework of bureaucracy that upholds and regulates education. Even though judges appear quick to make minor modifications involving religious prayers and exercises in non-denominational schools, they are reluctant to make decisions that will result in substantial changes to the overall infrastructure of the educational system itself, save for minority language rights issues which is clearly acknowledged by the judiciary as being a political mandate.

Aside from court orders mandating tangible and observable changes in schools, such as the elimination of religious curricula from some schools, or the creation of French sections within some school boards, there remains the underlying issue of how judicial interpretations affect administrative practices and school culture, in particular, and Canadian society at large.

A Comprehensive View of the Impact of the *Charter* in Education

Public schools are increasingly adopting a secular and non-sectarian perspective. State authorized religious instruction in non-constitutionally protected schools is increasingly seen as an impermissible imposition of religious beliefs. As a result, religious exercises and Christian practices that are given predominance over others, in particular, are no longer acceptable. Although the tradition of teaching and modelling one set of values is becoming increasingly taboo within school systems throughout the nation, the value of education as both a private and public good is seen as legitimate grounds for the state's controlling education of the young.

Legally, children must attend school and the existing infrastructures which regulate education are deemed secular in nature and not violative of religious freedoms. And it would be naive to believe that the central value (the worth of education) does not carry with it a host of formally and informally approved values. The formal values notably include bilingualism and, equally notably, exclude religion. Insofar as the elimination of Judeo-Christian values does leave a values vacuum, one may reasonably expect it to be filled with a passing array of politically favoured value preferences, such as environmentalism and responsible consumerism in these austere economic times (as recent down-sizing initatives have demonstrated).

The *Charter* maintains the *status quo* for certain denominational and separate schools. They currently enjoy considerable privileges which have arisen out of the guarantees accorded to them at Confederation. That is to say, Roman Catholic schools in many provinces now have protected special privileges, compared with other religious minorities, when in 1867 they were merely granted a continuity of the *status quo*, being the only significant minority at the time. What was minimally discriminatory in 1867, without a *Charter*, has become a major area of discrimination, undisturbed, and indeed reinforced, by the *Charter*.

On the other hand, the *status quo* has been greatly altered for French minority groups, extending well beyond legal minimalism. The "remedial provision" under section 23 of the *Charter* ultimately serves to protect, and indeed promote, minority language educational rights. This is currently being reinforced by general provincial legislation to assure "equal and just treatment" regarding education for both English and French minority language groups.

Further, school administrators are typically apprehensive when disciplining students because of fear, justified or unjustified, of legal implications and ambivalence about their decision-making autonomy under the *Charter* (Black-Branch, 1993a). Ironically, judges are generally upholding traditional administrative practices, and down-playing the rights and freedoms of students, parents and staff alike, in support of the reasonable management of schools. In many respects the courts are vesting legal authority in principals. For this reason many experts see administrative fears (a phenomenon which the author calls *Charter*-chill, see Appendix III) as being ill-founded. Such fears, however, may be more easily understood in view of the importance principals place on avoiding court actions. Winning a legal case is of little consequence to them if, in the process, they lose the respect of their community and possibly opportunities of promotion and career advancement.

In addition, the multicultural make-up of Canada is increasingly reflected, at a superficial level, in the day-to-day routines and curricula in most school systems. Similarly, a number of affirmative action programmes encourage women and people from a variety of ethnic backgrounds to apply for positions of added responsibility in education. As well, there is increased support for special education students. The motivation behind changes instituted in schools and school systems regarding multiculturalism, affirmative action programmes and special education is not ideologically clear. There is much stronger affirmation of minorities' rights to participate fully in a secular system than there is of their rights to maintain their own identity. An analogous ambivalence is found in aboriginal education where rights to educational autonomy and self-government are matched, or exceeded, by rights preparation for full participation in the national economy. There is some inconsistency between these parallel sets of alleged rights.

Judges Assuming a Political Role

Overall, the courts seem to be adopting a political, even a legislative or executive role, as distinct from providing a consistent interpretation of the *Charter*. Where there is apparent political will, the courts appear willing to provide the force, for example, to assure francophone schools for minorities and to ban mandatory religious practices and instruction. But the courts appear reluctant to advance the causes of minorities lacking wide political support and clout.

A Judicial Ideological Tug-of-War: Two Ideological Frameworks

These court decisions regarding education undoubtedly advance certain ideological perspectives. Whilst some courts have advanced particularly liberal views, others have been quite conservative. The difficulty with these terms is they are subject to interpretation. The terms liberal and conservative, in reference to judicial ideology, can be viewed within what the author sees as two predominant frameworks of judicial decision-making, the first is what he calls the societal-contextual framework, the second being the codified-interpretative framework.

Societal-Contextual Framework of Judicial Decision-Making

In the first framework, courts weigh the societal context as an important element in reaching their decisions. Liberal court decisions are described as those which protect individual rights above all else. Democracy is viewed as protecting all people even if it means denying the rights of the majority. Examples of these rulings would be the cases involving religion in *Zylberberg*, *Russow*, and *Elgin*. In *Elgin*, the Court explicitly stated that the minority could no longer be subjected to the tyranny of the majority. (See Table 9.1 below)

On the other hand, conservative rulings, within this framework also weigh the arguments within a specific societal context. In this instance, however, the judiciary protects the rights of the community at large, or a valued sub-community. They weigh the *Charter* in terms of being for the greatest good for the promotion of "peace, order and good government" and the maintenance of community. Decisions of this nature would be in the cases of *Jones, Cromer* and *Keegstra*. In *Jones*, the Supreme Court of Canada ruled that the school system is for the education of the young and indeed is a legitimate system. The Court upheld Cromer's being charged for a breach of the British Columbia Teachers' Code of Ethics for publicly criticizing a colleague. Both Keegstra and Ross were denied their individual freedom of speech for promoting hatred against the Jews. These are all conservative decisions that are seen as protecting society at large. (See Table 9.1 below)

Table 9.1:   Societal-Contextual Framework of Judicial Decision-Making

Type of Ruling	Ideology Behind the Ruling
Liberal Rulings	Protection of the Weakest
Conservative Rulings	Protection of the Community-at-Large

Codified-Interpretative Framework of Judicial Decision-Making

According to the second framework, the codified-interpretative framework, liberal courts not only continue their traditional role of interpreting legislation, but they accept their new power to scrutinize and strike down laws to be of "no force or effect". Conservative courts are reluctant to go beyond the legislative intent. Although the rulings in this framework may seem similar to those in the first camp, they are substantially different. The Court strictly follows its role (as interpreter and scrutineer of laws), viewing the *Charter* as codified principles of law that co-exist with other elements within the *Constitution Act*.

Liberal decisions involve the courts using their vested power and creativity in the capacity of a law-maker by striking down laws. They specify what has to be done and how it should be attained. Examples of this include the decisions in *Mahé* and *Marchand*. In *Mahé* the Court outlined the "sliding scale" approach for boards of education to follow regarding instruction, facilities and governance of minority language education. In *Marchand*, the Court ordered Simcoe County Board of Education to provide industrial arts and shop facilities and the necessary equipment to go with these facilities. The Court specified in no uncertain terms that such facilities and equipment had to be equivalent to that of the majority (anglophone) schools. In other words, the Court interpreted the meaning of the *Charter* in terms of its specific wording. In its ruling, it virtually legislated what had to be done to remedy the situation. (See Table 9.2 below)

Conservative rulings under this framework are once again rooted in following the exact wording of the *Charter*. An example of a conservative ruling is the *Adler* case. In this case, the Court initially used the limitations clause under section 1 of the *Charter* to justify the legitimacy of funding Roman Catholic schools in Ontario but not extending funding to other religious-based schools. According to the *Charter* and the Constitution as a whole, this was legitimate and would therefore remain. The Court clearly stated that this was a matter too important for the judiciary to decide, hence relying on the American political doctrine to send the issue back to the applicants to have Parliament decide. The Court of Appeal went beyond this stating that there was no breach of these rights in the first place.

This decision has been upheld by the Supreme Court of Canada (*Adler* (1997), discussed in Chapter 7). Here the Supreme Court stated that, "[s]ection 93 of the Constitution Act, 1867 is the product of a[n] historical compromise crucial to Confederation . . . which cannot be enlarged through the operation of . . . the *Charter*. . . . The province remains free to exercise its plenary power with regard to education in whatever way it sees fit, subject to the restrictions relating to separate schools imposed by s[ection] 93(1) ". (See Table 9.2 below)

Table 9.2: **Codified-Interpretative Framework of Judicial Decision-Making**

Type of Ruling	Ideology Behind the Ruling
Liberal Rulings	Change Agent: Strike Down Legislation
Conservative Rulings	Change Agent: Refer Issue Back to Government

Maintaining the Political *Status Quo*

Using either ideological framework, it is difficult to apply liberal or conservative labels to the sum of court rulings regarding the *Charter of Rights and Freedoms*. Some court decisions appear to be liberal within one framework, and others appear conservative within another framework. Whilst there appears to be no pattern or consistency by these two frameworks to these rulings, there is, indeed, a common thread.

Many rulings appear to be based on élite political sentiment whereby the judiciary upholds political ideology, be it in the area of secularizing the curriculum in non-denominational schools; continuing the privileges of religious schools protected under section 93 of the *Constitution Act 1867*; or promoting dual language school systems for minority language rightholders throughout the country. Such a model is what may be referred to as the political paradigm of judicial decision-making. (See Table 9.3 below)

The Political Paradigm of Judicial Decision-Making

It seems that judges pick and choose which framework they will use, consciously or unconsciously, in reaching their decisions in a given case. The only consistency to such choices appears to be that decisions are usually based on the dominant political ideology of the day.   In other words, they support the political *status quo*. That is, they either maintain the existing structures, such as with religious schools under section 93 of the *Constitution Act* 1867, or they re-align the system to suit the dominant political ideology of the day, such as in the case of minority language educational rights under section 23 of the *Charter*.

As a result Canadians see, *inter alia*: support for minority language educational rights;   support for the denominational system (protected under section 93 and section 29), paralleled by support for a non-religious school system;   and, support for multiculturalism, all of which are well-entrenched Government policies espoused by political élites.

Table 9.3:   The Political Paradigm of Judicial Decision-Making

Societal-Contextual Framework	Codified-Interpretative Framework
Liberal Rulings *Societal-Contextual*	*Liberal Rulings* *Codified-Interpretative*
Protection of the Weakest	**Change Agent: Strike Down Legislation**
Conservative Rulings *Societal-Contextual*	*Conservative Rulings* *Codified-Interpretative*
Protection of the Community at Large	**Change Agent: Refer Issue Back to Government**

The quilt-like body of *Charter* and education related case law is based on the pragmatic political situation of the time.   The Canadian judiciary makes rulings that secularize schools;   that limit freedom of religion and speech;   that extend the minority language educational rights of francophones; and, that uphold the existence of a Roman Catholic school system, which many would say effectively, "discriminates" against other religious groups. It is difficult to see any strong liberal or conservative principle at work by either framework.

In essence, the courts legitimate political ideology by galvanizing political will into jurisprudence. It will not breathe life into the *Charter* unless it sees a clear political mandate to do so. As a result, it is understandable if those who oppose judicial decisions sometimes see the courts as carrying out a political mandate -- out of reach of the electorate.

Conclusion: The *Charter* and Social Justice

With the institution of the *Charter* in 1982, Bora Laskin, then Chief Justice of Canada, recognized the potential of a wider role for judges under the *Charter*. At that time he questioned whether the courts would indeed "seize" this new role (The National, Laskin, 1984). More than a decade later, it would seem from the case law presented throughout this book that the Canadian judiciary has indeed seized its new power to scrutinize laws. But in doing so, it has not seized the opportunity to apply the *Charter* fully as an instrument of human rights, but merely to induce political correctness by effectively galvanizing political will into jurisprudence.

This author would contend that the Canadian judiciary is not applying the *Charter* to education for the advancement of egalitarian principles of social justice but, simply to maintain the political *status quo*, and effectively to re-align it where deemed necessary by political élites. As a result there is a continued and growing protection of certain groups, what the author calls élitist minorities, and the marginalization of others, disenfranchized minorities, under the new Canadian régime.

Epilogue

I have written this book primarily to inform those involved in education of the influence and implications of the *Canadian Charter of Rights and Freedoms*. I have tried to make it useful by summarizing practical suggestions for the administrator and by highlighting important cases to those interested in education and law. I have also tried to interpret the thrust of the courts' treatment of the *Charter* to promote understanding, discussion and future directions.

Throughout, I have been influenced by my own personal philosophy with respect to human rights and their codification. I am a strong believer in the clear expression of individual human rights and believe that the *Charter*, whilst not perfect, is a major, progressive step in the development of Canada's Constitution. At the same time, my reading of the jurisprudence has led to some disappointment. Too often the *Charter* has been used to advance the ideological interests of the élites, rather than as a check on those élites to the advantage of the individual.

Given our history, I believe that these basic rights and fundamental freedoms are best protected under international, and national laws that are politically endorsed, judicially monitored and enforced. Such laws should be beyond the reach of elected politicians and must be upheld in accordance with principles of fairness and impartiality and not that of popular political ideology.

No doubt no right is absolute. There must be a margin of appreciation of such rights and freedoms in that they are to be interpreted within a societal context whereby they are not exercised in a manner which is destructive to the broader international community. But with rights also come responsibilities.

References

L'Actualité. (1992, 1er octobre) "De la pauvreté de la pensée nationalist au Québec", *L'Actualité* [Québec].

Bercuson, D. & Wertheimer, D. (1987) *A Trust Betrayed: The Keegstra Affair*. Toronto: McClelland-Bantam.

Black's Law Dictionary (5th ed.) (1979) St. Paul: West Publishing.

Black-Branch, J. L. (1991) *Teachers' Working Conditions in Canada*. Council of Ministers of Education, Toronto, Canada.

Black-Branch, J. L. (1992a) *Religious Instruction and the Tyranny of the Christian Majority*. Paper presented to the Association for Moral Education, Ontario Moral/Values Education Association and Ontario Council in Educational Administration, Toronto, Canada.

Black-Branch, J. L. (1992b) *Minority Language Educational Rights: A Constitutional Right In Canada*. A paper presented at the VIIIth World Congress of Comparative Education, Prague, Czechoslovakia.

Black-Branch, J. L. (1992c) *Minority Language Rights: A Canadian Example*. Paper presented at the European Conference on Educational Research, Enschede, The Netherlands.

Black-Branch, J. L. (1992d) *Recognising Minority Language Educational Rights In A Reemergent Canada: Marchand v. Simcoe County Board of Education*. Paper presented for the Canadian Society for the Study of Education, Charlottetown, P.E.I., Canada.

Black-Branch, J. L. (1993a) *Traditions Rights and Realities: Legal,* de facto *and Symbolic Influences of the* Canadian Charter of Rights and Freedoms *on Educational Administration in Canada.* Unpublished doctoral dissertation at the University of Toronto.

Black-Branch, J. L. (1993b) Judicial Intervention, the Balancing of Interests and Administrative Decision-Making: Using the Canadian Charter of Rights and Freedoms as a Vehicle for Parental Participation in Settling Disputes Regarding Programme.   *Canadian Journal of Special Education Vol. 9, No. 1.*

Black-Branch, J. L. (1993c) O'Canada, Our Home on Native Land: Aboriginal Self Government May Be the Key to Educational Reform Not the Charter of Rights and Freedoms.   *The Canadian Journal of Native Studies, Vol. 13, No. 2.*

Black-Branch, J. L. (1994a) Weighing the Balance Between Constitutional Legal Rights and Administrative Duties.   *The Canadian Administrator, Vol. 33, No. 8, May.*

Black-Branch, J. L. (1994b) Fallen on Deaf Ears: A Legal Analysis of the Closure of the R. J. D. Williams Provincial School for the Deaf. *ACEHI Journal, Vol. 20, Issue 1/2.*

Clarkson, S. & McCall, C. (1990) *Trudeau and Our Times,   Volume 1: The Magnificient Obsession.* Toronto: McClelland & Stewart.

Cruickshank, D. (1986) Charter Equality Rights: The Challenge to Education Law and Policy.   In Michael E. Manley-Casimir & Terri A. Sussel (Eds.).   *Courts in the Classroom: Education and the Charter of Rights and Freedoms.*   Calgary: Detselig Enterprises.

Dickinson, G. M. (1992) Exploding the Myth . . . One More Time. *Education and Law Journal, 4.* Toronto: Carswell.

Dickinson, G. M. & MacKay, A. W. (1989) *Rights, Freedoms and the Education System in Canada/Cases and Materials.* Toronto: Emond-Montgomery.

Downey, L. W. (1988) *Policy Analysis in Education.* Calgary: Detselig Enterprises.

Gall, G. L. (1990) *The Canadian Legal System.* Toronto: Carswell.

Globe and Mail. (1992, April 17) "How the *Charter* changes justice", *The [Toronto] Globe and Mail.*

Globe and Mail. (1992, November 25) "Revolutionary-change agent", *The [Toronto] Globe and Mail.*

Globe and Mail. (1994, September 8) "Keegstra conviction struck down", *The [Toronto] Globe and Mail.*

Holmes, M. (1992) *Religion and Restructuring Schools.* Paper presented at the International Conference: Restructuring Education: Choices and Challenges, at OISE, Toronto.

Hoy, W. K. & Miskel, C. G. (1987) *Educational Administration: Theory, Research and Practice.* Toronto: Random House.

Laskin, J., Greenspan, E., Dunlop, J. B. & Rosenberg, M. (Eds.) (1982) *The Canadian Charter of Rights and Freedoms.* Aurora, Ontario: Canada Law Book.

MacKay, A. W. (1984) *Education Law in Canada.* Toronto: Emond-Montgomery Publications.

Manley-Casimir, M. E. & Sussel, T. A. (1986) *Courts in the Classroom: Education and the Charter of Rights and Freedoms.* Calgary: Detselig Enterprises.

National, Laskin (1980 in an interview) "Laskin Seized Chance for Change", *The National*, April 1984.

Oxford Concise Dictionary of Law. (1990) (2nd ed.)   Oxford: Oxford University Press.

Tarnopolsky, W. S. & Beaudoin, G-A. (1982) *Canadian Charter of Rights and Freedoms Commentary*. Toronto: Carswell.

Trudeau, P. E. (1968) *A Canadian Charter of Human Rights*.   Ottawa: Queen's Printer.

van Dijk, P. & van Hoof, G. J. H. (1992) (2d. ed.) *Theory and Practice of the European Convention on Human Rights*.   Deventer: Kluwer.

Zuker, M. A. (1988) *The Legal Context of Education*.   Toronto: OISE Press-Guidance Centre.

Main Statutes and Legal Documents

Alberta Act, 4-5 Edw. Vll, c. 3, *1905* (Canada).

British North America Act 1867. Now named *Constitution Act 1867,* 1867, 30-31 Vict., c. 3 (U.K.).

Canada Act 1982 (U.K.), *1982,* c. 11.

Canadian Bill of Rights, R.S.C. *1970*, Appendix III.

Canadian Charter of Rights and Freedoms, Part I of the *Constitution Act 1982*, being Schedule B of the *Canada Act 1982* (U.K.), 1982, c. 11, Appendix I.

la Charter de la languge française (R.S.Q. 1977, v. C - 11).

Constitution Act 1867, 30-31 Vict., c. 3 (U.K.) [formerly *British North America Act 1867*].

Constitution Act 1982, Schedule B of Canada Act (U.K.) 1982, c. 11.

Criminal Code, R.S.C. *1985*, c. C-46.

Education Act, Revised Statutes of Ontario, 1980 Chapter 129, April 1991.

Employment Equity Act 1988.

Manitoba Act 1870, 33 Vict., c. 3 (Canada)

Multicultural Act 1986.

Terms of Union of Newfoundland with Canada (confirmed by the *Newfoundland Act,* 12-13 Geo. Vl, c. 22 (U.K.)).

Saskatchewan Act, 4-5 Edw. Vll, c. 42, *1905* (Canada).

Young Offenders Act, R.S.C. *1985.*

Cases

Adler v. Ontario [1997] Unpublished documents of the Supreme Court of Canada rulings (File No.: 24347); *Elgersma v. Ontario (Attorney-General)* (1994) 116 D.L.R. (4th)) 1 (Ont. C.A.); (1992), 94 D.L.R. 417 (4th) (Div. Ct.).

Andrews v. Law Society (British Columbia) [1989] 1 S.C.R. 143, 2 W.W.R. 289, 56 D.L.R. (4th) 1 (S.C.C.).

Attorney General of Québec v. Greater Hull School Board et al. [1984] 2 S.C.R. 575, 15 D.L.R. (4th) 651.

Attorney General of Quebec v. Lavigne [1983] C.A. 370, rev'g (1981) 133 D.L.R. (3d) 606.

Bachmann v. St. James-Assiniboia School Division 2 (1984), 13 D.L.R. (4th) 606 (Man. C.A.).

Bal v. Ontario (Attorney General) (1994) 21 O.R. (3d) 681.

Bales v. Board of School Trustees (Central Okanagan) (1984), 54 B.C.L.R.

Black v. Metropolitan Separate School Board (1988), 29 O.A.C. 121 (Div. Ct.).

Caldwell v. Stuart [1984] 2 S.C.R. 603, 15 D.L.R. (4th) 1.

Casagrande v. Hinton Roman Catholic District No. 155 et al. (1987), 51 Alta. L.R. (2d) 349, 38 D.L.R. (4th) 382 (Alta. Q.B.).

Chaddock v. Mystery Lake School District 2355 [1986], 5 W.W.R. 673. Leave to appeal to the S.C.C. refused [1987] 1xviii [Man.].

Commission des Écoles Fransaskoises Inc. et al. v. Government of Saskatchewan [1988] 3 W.W.R. 354, 48 D.L.R. (4th). 315 (Sask. Q.B.).

Commission des Écoles Fransaskoises et al. v. Government of Saskatchewan (1991) 92 Sask. R. 267 (Sask. C.A.). Leave to appeal to the S.C.C. refused (1991), 97 Sask. R. 95.

Re: Constitutional Questions Act, etc. (Manitoba) [1990] 2 W.W.R. 289, 64 Man. R. (2d) 1(C.A.).

Corporation of the Canadian Civil Liberties Association v. Ontario (Ministry of Education) (1990), 71 O.R. (2d) 341 (C.A.).

Cromer v. British Columbia Teacher's Federation [1986] 5 W.W.R. 638 (B.C.C.A.).

Desmarais v. Morrissette (1991) [Unreported].

Devereux v. Lambton County (Roman Catholic Separate School Board) (September 1, 1988), Doc. No. RE 1544/88 (H.C.).

Eaton v. Brant County Board of Education [1997] Unpublished documents of the Supreme Court of Canada rulings (File No.: 24668); (1995) 22 O.R. (3d) 1. (Ont. C.A.).

Elwood v. Halifax (County) Bedford (District) School Board, (N.S.S.C.) October, 1986 (Interlocutory Injunction). Filed in the Supreme Court of Nova Scotia. The suit ended in Settlement Minutes dated 1 June 1987.

Re Essex County Roman Catholic Separate School Board and Porter [1978], 29 O.R. (2d) 255, 89 D.L.R. (3d) 445 (C.A.).

Ford v. Attorney General of Québec [1988] 2 S.C.R. 1, 54 D.L.R. (4th) 577.

Re Germany and Rauca (1983) 41 O.R. (2d) 225.

Goudreau v. Falher Consolidated School District No. 69 (1993), 8 Alta. L.R. (3d) (Alta. C.A.).

Griffin v. Commission Scolaire Regionale Blainville Deux-Montagnes et al. (1989), 63 D.L.R. (4th) 37 (Quebec Superior Court).

Hardy v. Minister of Education (1985) 67 B.C.L. 203 (S.C.).

Ignatescu v. Board of Education of Assiniboia School Division No. 69.

Jacobi v. Newell No.4 (County) et al. (1992) 136 A.R. 165 (Alta. Ct. Q.B.).

Jacobi v. Board of Education of Aqueduct Roman Catholic Separate School District No. 37 (1994) 150 A.R. 34 (Alta. Ct. Q.B.).

Jonson v. County of Ponoka #3 (1988), 12 C.R.D. 400 (Alta. Q.B.).

Keegstra v. Lacombe County 14 (Board of Education) (1983) 25 Alta. L.R. (2d) 370 (Bd. of Ref.).

Lanark, Leeds & Grenville Roman Catholic Separate School Board v. Ontario (Human Rights Commission), (sub nom. Hickling v. Lanark, Leeds & Grenville Roman Catholic Separate School Board) (1986), 7 C.H.R.R. D/3546 (Ont. Bd. of Inquiry), reversed (1987), 8 C.H.R.R. D/4235 60 O.R. (2d) 441, 40 D.L.R. (4th) 316, 24 O.A.C. 11 (Ont. Div. Ct.), affirmed (1989), 67 O.R. (2d) 479, 57 D.L.R. (4th) 479, 10 C.H.R.R.D/6336 (C.A.).

Lavoie et al. v. Attorney-General of Nova Scotia (1989), 91 N.S.R. (2d) 184, (1989) 58 D.L.R. (4th) 293 (C.A.).

Leshner v. Ontario (1992) Ontario Human Rights Board of Inquiry, judgment dated August 31, 1992: Toronto.

Lewis v. Burnaby School District No. 41 (1992), 68 B.C.L.R. (2d) 247 71 B.C.L.R.(2d) 183.

Lutes v. Board of Education of Prairie View School Division No. 74
(1992) 101 Sask. R. (Sask. Ct. Q.B.).

Mahé et al. v. R. in Right of Alberta et al. [1987] 6 W.W.R 331, 42
D.L.R. (4th) 514 (Alta. C.A.), rev'd [1990] 3 W.W.R. 97, 72
Alta. L.R. (2d) 257 (S.C.C.).

*Manitoba Association for Rights and Liberties et al. v. the Government of
Manitoba et al.* (1992) 82 M.R. (2d) 39 (Man. Ct. of Q.B.).

Marchand v. Simcoe County Board of Education et al. (1986), 55 O.R.
(2d) 638, 29 D.L.R. (4th) 596 (H.C.).

Marquardt v. Peace River South School District 59 (1990) (British
Columbia Human Rights Council).

*Re Maw et al. and Board of Education for the Borough of Scarborough et
al.* (1983), 43 O.R. (2d) 694 (H.C.).

*McIntyre v. The Public School Trustees of Section Eight in the Township
of Blanchard et al.* (1886), 11 O.R. 439 (County Ct.).

McNeil v. Nova Scotia Board of Censors [1978] 2 S.C.R. 662, 84 D.L.R.
(3d) 1.

*Re Metropolitan Toronto Board of Education et al. v. Attorney General for
Ontario* (1987), 10 C.R.D. 375.30-02 (S.C.C.).

Murdock v. Richards [1954] 1 D.L.R. 766 (N.S.S.C.).

*Newfoundland Teachers' Association et al. v. H.M. The Queen in Right of
Newfoundland et al.* (1988), 13 C.R.D. 375.30 - 01 (C.A.).

*Re Nova Scotia Teachers' Union et al. and the Attorney-General of Nova
Scotia; Nova Scotia Government Employees Union, Intervener*
(1993), 102 D.L.R. (4th) 267 (N.S.S.C.).

Noyes v. Board of School Trustees, District No. 30 (South Cariboo) (1985), 64 B.C.L.R. 287 (S.C.).

Ogg-Moss v. R. [1984] 2 S.C.R. 173, 111 D.L.R. (4th) 549 (S.C.C.).

Ontario English Catholic Teachers' Association v. Essex County Roman Catholic Separate School Board (1987), 36 D.L.R. (4th) 115 (Ont. Div. Ct.).

Ontario (Human Rights Commissioner) v. Peel (Board of Education) (1991), School Law Commentary, Case 6-1-1. Leave to the Ont. C.A. refused 3 O.R. (2d) 531n.

Ottawa Roman Catholic Separate School Trustees v. Ottawa [1917] A.C. 76 (P.C.).

Re Peel Board of Education and B et al. (1987) 59 O.R. (2d) 654, 24 Admin. L.R. 14 (H.C.).

Re Peel Board of Education v. B. (W.) (1990), (Ont. S. C.).

Piette v. Sault Ste. Marie Board of Education (10 November 1989), Algoma 2731/89 (H.C.).

Quebec Association of Protestant School Boards v. Attorney-General of Quebec [1984] 2 S.C.R. 66, 10 D.L.R. (4th) 321.

R. v. Arbeau (1986), 8 C.R.D. 375 (Nfld. C.A.).

R. v. B.C.W. (1986), 40 Man. R. (2d) 216 (Man. C.A.).

R. v. Bienert (1985), 6 C.R.D. 525.90 (Alta. Prov. Ct.).

R. v. Boone (1989), 229 A.P.R. 141 (Nfld. Prov. Ct).

R. v. Cline (1988), (Sask. Prov. Ct.) [Unreported].

R. v. Dimmell (1980), 55 C.C.C. (2d) 239 (Ont. Dist. Ct.).

R. Drybones [1970] S.C.R. 282.

R. v. Edwards Books and Art Ltd. [1986] 28 C.R.R. 1, 2 S.C.R. 713.

R. v. G. (James Michael) (1986), 56 O.R. (2d) 705 (C.A.). Leave to appeal to S.C.C. refused (1987), 59 O.R. (2d) 286 (note) (S.C.C.).

R. v. J. R. G. (1991), 22 C.R.D. 800 (B.C. Youth Ct.).

R. v. Gaul (1904), 36 N.S.R. 504 (C.A.).

R. v. Haberstock (1970), 1 C.C.C. (2d) 433 (Sask. C.A.).

R. v. Jomaa (1987), 11 C.R.D. 125 (Albt. Prov. Ct.).

R. v. Jones [1986] 2 S.C.R. 284, 31 D.L.R. (4th) 569.

R. v. Jones (1987) 84 A.R. 141 (Alta. Prov. Ct.).

R. v. Keegstra [1984] 19 C.C.C. (3d) 254 (Alta. Q.B.).

R. v. Keegstra (1990) 19 C.R.D. 775; 114 A. R. 81 (S.C.C.).

R. v. Keegstra (1994) Doc. Calgary Appeal 13537 (Alta. C.A.).

R. v. Kind (1984), 50 Nfld. & P.E.I. 332, 5 C.R.D. 125 (Nfld. Dist. Ct.).

R. v. Kotelmach and Kotelmach (1989) 76 Sask. R. 116 (Sask. Q.B.).

R. v. Lauzon (23 May 1991), (Ont. Prov. Div.), Merredew Prov. J. [Unreported].

R. v. McCloud and Randell (1987), 10 C.R.D. 375 (S. C. Nfld.).

R. v. Metcalfe (1927), 49 C.C.C. 260 (Sask. Dist. Ct.).

R. v. Nelson (1989), (Ont. Dist Ct.) [Unreported], rev'd in part (1989), 51 C.C.C. (3d) 150 (Ont. H.C.).

R. v. Oakes [1986] 1 S.C.R. 103, 26 D.L.R. (4th) 200 (S.C.C.).

R. v. Powell et al. (1985), 6 C.R.D. 125 (Albt. Prov. Ct.).

R. v. Prentice (1985), 6 C.R.D. 775 (Ont. Prov. Ct.).

R. v. Stymiest (1993), 79 C.C.C. (3d) 408 (B.C.C.A.).

R. v. Sweet (12 December 1986), (Ont. Dist. Ct.) [Unreported].

R. v. Turpin [1989] 1 S.C.R. 1296, 48 C.C.C. (3d) 8; 22 O. R. (3d) 13; C.R.R. 306.

R. v. W. and B. (1990), 18 C.R.D. 850.60 (S.C. Nfld.).

Reference Re An Act to Amend the Education Act [1987] 1 S.C.R. 1148, 40 D.L.R. (4th) 18 (S.C.C.).

Reference Re Education Act of Ontario and Minority Language Educational Rights (1984), 47 O.R. (2d) 1, 10 D.L.R. (4th) 491 (C.A.).

Reference Re Education Act (Quebec) (1993) 154 N.R. (S.C.C.).

Reference re Public Schools Act (Manitoba) (1993), 100 D.L.R (4th).

Reference re Minority Language Educational Rights (P.E.I.) (March 4, 1988) (P.E.I. C.A.).

Resort Village of Mitusinne v. Outlook School Division No. 32 (1989), 5 W.W.R. 710 (Sask. Q.B.).

Robichaud v. Nouveau-Brunswick (La Commission Scolaire No. 39) (1989), 99 N.B.R. (2d) 341 (C.A.), rev'g 95 N.B.R. (2d) 375, [1989] N.B.J. No. 49 (Q.B.).

Romaine v. Workers' Compensation Board (1988), 13 C.R.D. 125 (Alta. Ct. Q.B.).

Ross v. (New Brunswick) Moncton Board of School Trustees, District No. 15 (1993) 110 D.L.R. (4th) 241 (N.B.C.A.); [1996] S.C.J. No. 40, S.C.C..

Rowett v. York Region (Board of Education) (1986), (Regional Special Education Trib.), aff'd (1988), 63 O.R. (2d) 767 (H.C.), rev'd (1989), 69 O.R. (2d) 543 (C.A.).

Russow et al. v. British Columbia (Attorney General) (1989), 35 B.C.L.R. (2d) 29 (S.C).

Sehdev v. Bayview Glen Junior Schools Ltd. (March 11, 1988) 9 C.H.R.R. D/4881 (Ontario Human Rights Commission Board of Inquiry).

Serup v. Board of Trustees of School District # 57 et al. (1987), 39 D.L.R. (4th) 754 (B.C.S.C.).

Shewan v. Abbotsford School District 34 (1987), 47 D.L.R. (4th) 106 (B.C.C.A.).

Smith v. Attorney General of Nova Scotia (1989), 15 C.R.D. 475 (S.C. N.S.).

Société des Acadiens du Nouveau-Brunswick Inc. et al. v. Association Of Parents for Fairness in Education, Grand Falls District 50 Branch [1986] 1 S.C.R. 549, 27 D.L.R. (4th) 406 (S.C.C.).

Spier v. Burnaby Board of School Trustees, District No. 41 (1988), (B.C.S.C.) [Unreported].

St. John's School Tax Authority v. Winter (1990), 17 C.R.D. 350 (Nfld. Prov. Ct.).

Tiny Township Roman Catholic Separate School Trustees v. The King [1928] A.C. 363 (P.C.).

Tomen v. Federation of Women Teachers' Associations of Ontario (1987), 61 O.R. (2d) 489 (H.C.J.), aff'd (1989), 70 O.R. (2d) 48, 34 O.A.C. 343 (C.A.); leave to appeal to S.C.C. refused 3 O.R. (3d) xiii.

Trofimenkoff v. Saskatchewan Minister of Education (1991) 92 Sask. R. 235 (Sask. Q.B.); (1991) 97 Sask. R. 161 (Sask. C.A.).

Walsh and Newfoundland Teachers' Association v. Newfoundland (Treasury Board) and Federation of School Boards of Newfoundland (1988), 71 Nfld. & P.E.I.R. 21.

Re Ward and Board of Blaine Lake School Unit No. 57 [1971] 4 W.W.R 161; 20 DLR (3d) 651 (Sask.Q.B).

Warkentin et al. v. Sault Ste. Marie Board of Education et al., 49 C.P.C. 31 (Ont. Dist. Ct.)

Weinstein et al. v. Ministry of Education (British Columbia), [1985] 5 W.W.R. 724 (B.C.S.C.).

Whittington et al. v. Board of School Trustees of School District No. 63 (Saanich) (1987), 16 B.C. L.R. (2d) 255, 44 D.L.R. (4th) 128 (S.C.).

Zylberberg et al. v. The Director of Education of the Sudbury Board of Education (1988), 65 O.R. (2d) 641, 34 C.R.R. 1, 52 D.L.R. (4th), 29 O.A.C. 23 (C.A.).

Appendix I: The Canadian Charter of Rights and Freedoms

Constitution Act 1982
as enacted by the Canada Act 1982 (U.K.), c.11

PART I SCHEDULE B

Preamble
Whereas Canada is founded upon principles that recognize the supremacy
of God and the rule of law:

Guarantee of Rights and Freedoms
1. The *Canadian Charter of Rights and Freedoms* guarantees the rights
    and freedoms set out in it subject only to such reasonable limits
    prescribed by law as can be demonstrably justified in a free and
    democratic society.

Fundamental Freedoms
2   Everyone has the following fundamental freedoms:
    (a) freedom of conscience and religion;
    (b) freedom of thought, belief, opinion and expression, including
    freedom of the press and other media of communication;
    (c) freedom of peaceful assembly; and
    (d) freedom of association.

Democratic Rights
3. Every citizen of Canada has the right to vote in an election of
    members of the House of Commons or of a legislative assembly and
    to be qualified for membership therein.
4. (1) No House of Commons and no legislative assembly shall
    continue for longer than five years from the date fixed for the return
    of writs at a general election of its members.

4.   (2) In time of real or apprehended war, invasion or insurrection, a House of Commons may be continued by Parliament and a legislative assembly may be continued by the legislature beyond five years if such continuation is not opposed by the votes of more than one-third of the members of the House of Commons or the legislative assembly, as the case may be.

5.   There shall be a sitting of Parliament and of each legislature at least once every twelve months.

Mobility Rights

6.   (1) Every citizen of Canada has the right to enter, remain in and leave Canada.

6.   (2) Every citizen and every person who has the status of a permanent resident of Canada has the right
      (a) to move to and take up residence in any province; and
      (b) to pursue the gaining of a livelihood in any province.

6.   (3) The rights specified in subsection (2) are subject to
      (a) any laws or practices of general application in force in a province other than those that discriminate among persons primarily on the basis of province of present or previous residence; and
      (b) any laws providing for reasonable residency requirements as a qualification for the receipt of publicly provided social services.

6.   (4) Subsections (2) and (3) do not preclude any law, program or activity that has its object the amelioration in a province of conditions of individuals in that province who are socially or economically disadvantaged if the rate of employment in that province is below the rate of employment in Canada.

Legal Rights

7.   Everyone has the right to life, liberty and security of person and the right not to be deprived thereof except in accordance with the principles of fundamental justice.

8.   Everyone has the right to be secure against unreasonable search or seizure.

9.   Everyone has the right not to be arbitrarily detained or imprisoned.

10.   Everyone has the right on arrest or detention
      (a) to be informed promptly of the reasons therefore;

(b) to retain and instruct counsel without delay and to be informed of that right; and

(c) to have the validity of the detention determined by way of *habeas corpus* and to be released if the detention is not lawful.

11. Any person charged with an offence has the right

(a) to be informed without unreasonable delay of the specific offence;

(b) to be tried within a reasonable time;

(c) not to be compelled to be a witness in proceedings against that person in respect of the offence;

(d) to be presumed innocent until proven guilty according to law in a fair and public hearing by an independent and impartial tribunal;

(e) not to be denied reasonable bail without just cause;

(f) except in the case of an offence under military law tried before a military tribunal, to the benefit of trial by jury where the maximum punishment for the offence is imprisonment for five years or a more severe punishment;

(g) not to be found guilty on account of any act or omission unless, at the time of the criminal offence according to the general principles of law recognized by the community of nations;

(h) if finally acquitted of the offence, not to be tried for it again and, if finally found guilty and punished for the offence, not to be tried or punished for it again; and

(i) if found guilty of the offence and if the punishment for the offence has been varied between the time of commission and the time of sentencing, to the benefit of the lesser punishment.

12. Everyone has the right not to be subjected to any cruel and unusual treatment or punishment.

13. A witness who testifies in any proceedings has the right not to have any incriminating evidence so given used to incriminate that witness in any other proceedings, except in a prosecution for perjury or for the giving of contradictory evidence.

14. A party or witness in any proceedings who does not understand or speak the language in which the proceedings are conducted or who is deaf has the right to the assistance of an interpreter.

Equality Rights
15. (1) Every individual is equal before and under the law and has the right to the equal protection and equal benefit of the law without discrimination and, in particular, without discrimination based on race, national or ethnic origin, colour, religion, sex, age or mental or physical disability.
15. (2) Subsection (1) does not preclude any law, program or activity that has as its object the amelioration of conditions of disadvantaged individuals or groups including those that are disadvantaged because of race, national or ethnic origin, colour, religion, sex, age or mental or physical disability.

Official Languages of Canada
16. (1) English and French are the official languages of Canada and have equality of status and equal rights and privileges as to their use in all institutions of the Parliament and government of Canada.
16. (2) English and French are the official languages of New Brunswick and have equality of status and equal rights and privileges as to their use in all institutions of the legislature and government of New Brunswick.
16. (3) Nothing in this Charter limits the authority of Parliament or a legislature to advance the equality of status or use of English and French.
17. (1) Everyone has the right to use English or French in any debates and other proceedings of Parliament.
17. (2) Everyone has the right to use English or French in any debates and other proceedings of the legislature of New Brunswick.
18. (1) The statutes, records and journals of Parliament shall be printed and published in English and French and both language versions are equally authoritative.
18. (2) The statutes, records and journals of New Brunswick shall be printed and published in English and French and both language versions are equally authoritative.
19. (1) Either English or French may be used by any person in, or in any pleading in or process from, any court established by Parliament.
19. (2) Either English or French may be used by any person in, or in any pleading in or process from, any court of New Brunswick.
20. (1) Any member of the public in Canada has the right to

communicate with, and to receive available services from, any head or central office of an institution of the Parliament or government of Canada in English or French, and has the same right with respect to any other office of any such institution where (a) there is a significant demand for communications with and services from that office in such language; or (b) due to the nature of the office, it is reasonable that communications with and services from that office be available in both English and French.

20. (2) Any member of the public in New Brunswick has the right to communicate with, and to receive available services from, any office of an institution of the legislature or government of New Brunswick in English or French.

21. Nothing in sections 16 to 20 abrogates or derogates from any right, privilege or obligation with respect to English and French languages, or either of them, that exists or is continued by virtue of any other provision of the Constitution of Canada.

22. Nothing in sections 16 to 20 abrogates or derogates from any legal or customary right or privilege acquired or enjoyed either before or after the coming into force of this Charter with respect to any language that is not English or French.

Minority Language Education Rights

23 (1) Citizens of Canada
(a) whose first language learned and still understood is that of the English or French linguistic minority population of the province in which they reside, or
(b) who have received their primary school instruction in Canada in English or French and reside in a province where the language in which they received that instruction in the language is English or French linguistic minority population of the province, have the right to have their children receive primary and secondary school instruction in that language in that province.

23. (2) Citizens of Canada of whom any child has received or is receiving primary or secondary school instruction in English or French in Canada, have the right to have all their children receive primary and secondary school instruction in the same language.

23. (3) The right of citizens of Canada under subsections (1) and (2) to have their children receive primary and secondary school instruction

in the language of the English or French linguistic minority population of a province

(a) applies wherever in the province the number of children of citizens who have such a right is sufficient to warrant the provision to them out of public funds of minority language instruction; and

(b) includes, where the number of those children so warrants, the right to have them receive that instruction in minority language educational facilities provided out of public funds.

Enforcement

24. (1) Anyone whose rights or freedoms, as guaranteed by this Charter, have been infringed or denied may apply to a court of competent jurisdiction to obtain such remedy as the court considers appropriate and just in the circumstances.

24. (2) Where, in proceedings under subsection (1), a court concludes that evidence was obtained in a manner that infringed or denied any rights or freedoms guaranteed by this Charter, the evidence shall be excluded if it is established that, having regard to all the circumstances, the admission of it in the proceedings would bring the administration of justice into disrepute.

General

25. The guarantee in this Charter of certain rights and freedoms shall not be construed so as to abrogate or derogate from any aboriginal, treaty or other rights and freedoms that pertain to the aboriginal peoples of Canada including

(a) any rights or freedoms that have been recognized by the Royal Proclamation of October 7, 1763; and

(b) any rights or freedoms that may be acquired by the aboriginal peoples of Canada by way of land claims settlement.

26. The guarantee in this Charter of certain rights and freedoms shall not be construed as denying the existence of any other rights or freedoms that exist in Canada.

27. This Charter shall be interpreted in a manner consistent with the preservation and enhancement of the multicultural heritage of Canadians.

28. Notwithstanding anything in this Charter, the rights and freedoms referred in it are guaranteed equally to male and female persons.

29. Nothing in this Charter abrogates or derogates from any rights or privileges guaranteed by or under the Constitution of Canada in respect of denominational, separate or dissentient schools.
30. A reference in this Charter to a province or to the legislative assembly or legislature of a province shall be deemed to include a reference to the Yukon Territory and the Northwest Territories, or to the appropriate legislative authority thereof, as the case may be.
31. Nothing in this Charter extends the legislative powers of any body or authority.

Application of Charter
32 (1) This Charter applies
(a) to the Parliament and government of Canada in respect of all matters within the authority of Parliament including all matters relating to the Yukon Territory and Northwest Territories; and
(b) to the legislature and government of each province in respect of all matters within the authority of the legislature of each province.
32. (2) Notwithstanding subsection (1), section 15 shall not be in effect until three years after this section comes into force.
33. (1) Parliament or the legislature of a province may expressly declare in an Act of Parliament or of the legislature, as the case may be, that the Act or a provision thereof shall operate notwithstanding a provision included in section 2 or sections 7 to 15 of this Charter.
33. (2) An Act or provision of an Act in respect of which a declaration made this section is in effect shall have such operation as it would have but for the provision of this Charter referred to in the declaration.
33. (3) A declaration made under subsection (1) shall cease to have effect five years after it comes into force or on such earlier date as may be specified in the declaration.
33. (4) Parliament or the legislature of a province may re-act a declaration made under subsection (1).
33. (5) Subsection (3) applies in respect of a re-enactment made under subsection (4).

Citation
34. This Part may be cited as the *Canadian Charter of Rights and Freedoms*.

PART VII
GENERAL

52. (1) The Constitution of Canada is the supreme law of Canada, and any law that is inconsistent with the provisions of the Constitution is, to the extent of the inconsistency, of no force or effect.

Appendix II:
Canadian Bill of Rights

Canadian Bill of Rights
An Act for the Recognition and Protection of Human Rights and
Fundamental Freedoms

8-9 Elizabeth II, c. 44 (Canada)
[Assented to 10th August 1960]

The Parliament of Canada, affirming that the Canadian Nation is founded upon principles that acknowledge the supremacy of God, the dignity and worth of the human person and the position of the family in a society of free men and institutions;

Affirming also that men and institutions remain free only when freedom is founded upon respect for moral and spiritual values and the rule of law;

And being desirous of enshrining these principles and the human rights and fundamental freedoms derived from them, in a Bill of Rights which shall reflect the respect of Parliament for its constitutional authority and which shall ensure the protection of these rights and freedoms in Canada:

Therefore Her Majesty, by and with the advice and consent of the Senate and House of Commons of Canada, enacts as follows:

PART I
BILL OF RIGHTS

1. It is hereby recognized and declared that in Canada there have existed and shall continue to exist without discrimination by reason of race, national origin, colour, religion or sex, the following human rights and fundamental freedoms, namely,

    (a) the right of the individual to life, liberty, security of the person and enjoyment of property, and the right not to be deprived thereof except by due process of law;

(b)   the right of the individual to equality before the law and the protection of the law;

(c)   freedom of religion;

(d)   freedom of speech;

(e)   freedom of assembly and association; and

(f)   freedom of the press.

2.   Every law of Canada shall, unless it is expressly declared by an Act of the Parliament of Canada that it shall operate notwithstanding the Canadian Bill of Rights, be so construed and applied as not to abrogate, abridge or infringe or to authorize the abrogation, abridgement or infringement of any of the rights or freedoms herein recognized and declared, and in particular, no law of Canada shall be construed or applied so as to

(a)   authorize or effect the arbitrary detention, imprisonment or exile of any person;

(b)   impose or authorize the imposition of cruel and unusual punishment;

(c)   deprive a person who has been arrested or detained

(i)   of the right to be informed promptly of the reason for his arrest or detention;

(ii)   of the right to retain and instruct counsel without delay, or

(iii) of the remedy by way of *habeas corpus* for the determination of the validity of his detention and for his release if the detention is not lawful;

(d)   authorize a court, tribunal, commission, board or other authority to compel a person to give evidence if he is denied counsel, protection against self incrimination or other constitutional safeguards;

(e)   deprive a person of the right to a fair hearing in accordance with the principles of fundamental justice for the determination of his rights and obligations;

(f)   deprive a person charged with a criminal offence of the right to be presumed innocent until proven guilty according to law in a fair and public hearing by an independent and impartial tribunal, or of the right to reasonable bail without just cause; or

(g)   deprive a person of the right to the assistance of an interpreter in any proceedings in which he is involved or in which he is a party or a witness, before a court, commission, board or other tribunal, if he does not understand or speak the language in which such proceedings are conducted.

3. (1)   Subject to subsection (2), the Minister of Justice shall, in accordance with such regulations as may be prescribed by the Governor in Council, examine every regulation transmitted to the Clerk of the Privy Council for registration pursuant to the *Statutory Instruments Act* and every Bill introduced in or presented to the House of Commons by a Minister of the Crown, in order to ascertain whether any of the provisions thereof are inconsistent with the purposes and provisions of this Part and he shall report any such inconsistency in the House of Commons at the first convenient opportunity.

(2) A regulation need not be examined in accordance with subsection (1) if prior to being made it was examined as a proposed regulation in accordance with subsection 3 of the *Statutory Instruments Act* to ensure that it was not inconsistent with the purposes and provisions of this Part.[1]

4.   The provisions of this Part shall be known as the *Canadian Bill of Rights*.

PART II

5. (1)   Nothing in Part I shall be construed to abrogate or abridge any human right or fundamental freedom not enumerated therein that may have existed in Canada at the commencement of this Act.

(2) The expression "law of Canada" in Part I means an Act of Parliament of Canada enacted before or after the coming into force of this Act, any order, rule or regulation thereunder, and any law in force in Canada or in any part of Canada at the commencement of this Act that is subject to be repealed, abolished or altered by the Parliament of Canada.

(3) The provisions of Part I shall be construed as extending only to matters coming within the legislative authority of the Parliament of Canada.

[1]   Section 3 was repealed and replaced by S.C. 1985, c. 26, s. 105.

Appendix III:
Charter-Related Change

The author (as discussed in Black-Branch; 1993a) states that there are three possible causes of educational change under the *Charter*, namely:
(1) legal changes (via judicial orders and judicial interpretation);
(2) symbolic changes (via *Charter*-Chill and the Halo-Effect); and,
(3) *de facto* changes.

(1) Legal Changes: Judicial Orders and Judicial Interpretation

Many changes to existing educational policies and practices have resulted from litigation (judicial orders and judicial interpretation). Judicial rulings and specific court orders act as legal authority to either uphold or change school policies. Judicial orders are not necessarily the same thing as judicial interpretations. Obviously judicial orders are direct change agents. Judicial interpretations (including their results, i.e., court orders) can also indirectly cause change in other analogous areas by providing a warning (prediction) about how courts would view certain policies or practices, if challenged. Essentially, the courts are one impetus of change regarding the *Charter* and education and legal changes under the *Charter* form the basis of this particular book.

(2) Symbolic Change: *Charter*-Chill and the Halo-Effect

Symbolic change means that the perceptions people (such as policy-makers and administrators) have about the *Charter* (whether legally sensible or not) can result in the creation of a new set of assumptions about rights, duties, power, relationships, expectations, etc., in turn resulting in policy and practice change -- called enhanced rights consciousness. The *Charter* is the symbol of such a consciousness.

In other words, certain policies within a school or school system may be amended or instituted simply because the *Charter* is seen, correctly or not, as a force that commands such changes. That is to say, the perceived symbolism or meaning of the *Charter* itself becomes the impetus of change. As a result, policies and practices are altered to accommodate myths because people internalize new meanings that are not necessarily legitimate. Two types of symbolic changes are what the author calls *Charter*-Chill and the Halo-Effect.

Charter-Chill

Charter-Chill is a symbolic negative perception where people are afraid of the *Charter*. *Charter*-Chill usually leads to changes in policy and practice which are often unwarranted as the *Charter* has been misinterpreted and misrepresented. The threat of litigation, for example, may prompt unfounded myths and fears which result in school systems changing certain policies.

Halo-Effect

The second type of symbolism involves the positive perception, or the Halo-Effect of the *Charter*. Some people see the *Charter* as a vehicle for doing good. They believe that the underlying principles of this document are for the advancement of humanity. Some schools, for example, have instituted racism awareness curricula to advance notions of equality and multiculturalism. In these instances, the *Charter* is used (rightly or wrongly) to institute changes which are positive.

(3) *De facto* Changes

De facto changes are changes made in legislation, policies and practices by informed individuals who know a violation of the *Charter* exists. *De facto*, or informed, changes are part of a regularized process of wholesale review and changes to policies and practices made to conform to the

Charter. In these instances, although not officially sanctioned, operating policies were revised to be consistent with *Charter* provisions. Revisions of this nature are made usually to avoid potential litigation and are legally grounded. Legislative amendments made to clean up statutes which may have invoked litigation are examples of *de facto* changes. These changes have been the impetus of many changes in schools and school systems.

Index

moral purposes, 150
morality, 40, 46, 150, 151
more rights conscious, 17
mosaic, 13, 169
Mulroney, Brian, 29, 138
multicultural, 13, 36, 58, 63, 163, 164,
    165, 166, 168, 169, 177
Multicultural Act, 163
multicultural diversity, 13
multiculturalism, 58, 163, 164, 165,
    167, 168, 177, 182
multi-denominational, 58
Muslim, 45, 58, 93

—N—

narcotics, 72, 73, 74
national origin, 8
Native Council of Canada, 172
Nazi Germany, 4
New Brunswick, 61, 62, 106, 114, 127,
    141
New Brunswick *Human Rights Act*, 61
new Canadian régime, 183
Newfoundland, 50, 52, 74, 79, 97, 115,
    142, 144, 145, 146, 151, 152, 153,
    160
non-Christian, 39
non-denominational board system along
    linguistic lines, 156
non-denominational public schools, 28
non-denominational schools, 46, 63,
    150, 173, 174, 176, 181
non-obstanante, 23, 27
non-sectarian principles, 40
non-sectarian school system, 40
Northwest Territories, 20, 143, 144,
    151
notwithstanding clause, 23, 27, 28, 29,
    30, 36
Nova Scotia, 99, 100, 101, 104, 125,
    141
numbers warrant provision, 129

—O—

Oakes Test, 25
obedience, 65, 68
obligations of school boards for
    Catholics and Protestants, 155
observances, 38, 39, 40
Official Languages Act, 113
Ontario, 39, 40, 41, 42, 43, 44, 45, 46,
    51, 58, 63, 64, 66, 72, 75, 76, 77,
    80, 82, 83, 90, 94, 101, 105, 106,
    107, 108, 109, 120, 121, 122, 123,
    126, 133, 137, 141, 148, 149, 152,
    154, 157, 158, 160, 161, 167, 175,
    180
Ontario Court of Appeal, 46, 58, 105,
    107, 120, 157
Ontario Teachers' Federation, 80
opinion, 14, 32, 35, 38, 62, 106, 115
other religious-based schools and schools
    systems, 157

—P—

Pakistani, 92
paradox regarding the direction for
    improving aboriginal education, 173
parents, 19, 41, 45, 46, 49, 50, 51, 53,
    54, 55, 56, 63, 65, 67, 71, 81, 82,
    84, 87, 94, 97, 104, 105, 106, 107,
    108, 109, 110, 115, 119, 121, 124,
    125, 126, 127, 131, 134, 135, 153,
    168, 177
Parliament, 1, 3, 8, 9, 10, 11, 12, 14,
    15, 16, 20, 25, 27, 28, 113, 114,
    140, 141, 142, 180
parliamentary system of government, 1
patriating the Canadian constitution, 13
peace, order, and good government, 11
peace-keeper, 7
Pearson, Lester B., 12
pedagogy, 166, 167
Penetanguishene, 121, 123
personal criticism, 55, 56
personal preferences, 53, 96
physical force, 66, 67